MOTHER INDIA

RECIPES PICTURES STORIES

MOTHER INDIA

RECIPES PICTURES STORIES

BY MONIR MOHAMMED
AND MARTIN GRAY

preface

Contents

Monir in his
kitchen, at home.

Martin Gray studied Fine Art at Central Saint Martin's, London,
graduating in the 1990s. He has worked as a photographer and
occasional ghost-writer on a number of publications, notably illustrating one
of the *River Café Cook Books*. His photography has been exhibited across
the British Isles and overseas including a widely acclaimed solo show at
the Kelvingrove Art Gallery and Museum in Glasgow. Martin's personal
photographic project 'A Sideways Glance' is used in various contexts
around several different cities. Martin and Monir Mohammed, Chef-Proprietor
of Mother India, have collaborated over a number of years and
are now firm friends.

Introduction by Martin Gray

Indian food is one of the most varied, subtle and seasonal of the world's great cuisines — a fact sometimes overlooked on the hungry stroll to the nearest takeaway. I'm pretty sure the food in this book will open your eyes to its possibilities, under the guidance of a master.

As well as featuring some extraordinary recipes, this book takes a closer look, in words and pictures, at the deep connection between Indian restaurants and the cities and towns that surround them.

At its heart is the personal story of Monir Mohammed, the enormously talented chef behind the Mother India restaurants. Monir's is a well-worn path in the catering business, and one followed by many British-Asian kids. In Monir's case, the backdrop is central Scotland, but the story could be the same in Birmingham, Manchester, London, Dublin, or almost any city or town around the world. But it is what Monir learned in the Punjab in his twenties that has made his cooking so unique.

Monir and I both grew up in Glasgow, so the sense of place has been shared in similar and different ways. These high streets, trains and buses, dialects, tenements, housing estates, parks, cinemas and shops have been the backdrop of our youth — and, of course, so has food.

What we both took for granted was that kids from all sorts of backgrounds grew up around each other. Looking back, I realise this was great. People you share ideas and connections with come in all shapes and sizes, colours and creeds, and without that melting pot an outsider can feel much more alone, but with it, we can all learn from each other. Glasgow has never been as multi-cultural as London or New York, but it's very much a city with a long history of hard-working migrants. You don't have to look very far back in the vast majority of Glaswegian family trees to find ancestry from somewhere further north, south, east or west, even if it was just the other side of a few lochs.

What many of us agree on is that life would have been more boring without a wide variety of friends and neighbours, and a lot less tasty without curry.

My Danish mum and Glaswegian dad settled in Glasgow when my mum was about thirty, after getting married in Denmark. The fact that Dad's brave attempts at pronouncing Danish were greeted with bemusement or outright hilarity answered the question as to where we would live. So my brother Niels and I ended up being Scots rather than Danes. We spent so much time visiting Denmark that I remember being pretty confused at first as to where I was supposed to be from.

When I was about seven or eight we got new Indian neighbours and I became friends with their son Sundeep after my mum arranged for his beautiful big sister to walk us to school. Their mum always seemed to be working away in the kitchen, and when I finally got to taste the food I was hooked.

Sundeep himself seemed to take all these great dinners for granted, and the most excited I remember him being about anything food-related back then was his discovery of spearmint gum. One afternoon he rushed into our kitchen clutching this packet and saying, 'Martin, you've got to try this stuff … it's fantastic.' He then proceeded to give me a master-class on the correct way to eat it, which involved carefully rolling a strip into a tight coil before chewing. I was so sure this was the proper way of doing things that the first time I saw someone chucking an uncoiled strip into their mouth, I ran back to Sundeep's to tell him there were still people out there who obviously hadn't learned the correct technique.

Starting school in Glasgow with a kind of hybrid Danishy accent wasn't perhaps the best move on the popularity front. Our rather elderly teacher thought my accent was adorable, and kept sitting me on her knee and explaining this to the class, which didn't exactly help my cause.

Sundeep wasn't bothered, as he had a kind of hybrid accent himself. Another friend, Warren Deatcher, was an Asian kid adopted into a family of Celtic fans, on a street full of Rangers fans, so he had issues of his own to deal with. There's a well-worn anecdote from the 1980s about an Asian guy from Glasgow who goes down south to see his cousins in London. They ask him, 'How is it with the racism up there?' He replies, 'No bother, the Catholics and Protestants are all too busy winding each other up.' Thankfully Scotland has moved on a lot since then, but poor Warren seemed to be getting it from all angles for a bit, though everything settled down pretty quickly.

I didn't have Scotland's most successful career in the Boys' Brigade, as I kept daydreaming when I was supposed to be marching, and marching when I was supposed to have stopped marching. One day Warren came to the door and said, 'Come on, why don't you try the Cubs?' So off I went and I remember being welcomed by this happy band from all sorts of backgrounds with all sorts of strengths and weaknesses. I think it was the first time I felt I fitted in. I saw the best of Glasgow there: everyone appreciating each other, pulling together for some kind of greater good. The power of feeling accepted as a kid is huge, so for us this was some kind of Utopia.

I also got an early realisation of food being a great leveller. Back in my childhood, long before Scandinavia had become in any way trendy, or even on the map with your average household, Mum's filter coffee and homemade Danish pastries would melt the hearts and delight the mouths of the neighbours. Conversations would spark up. Niels and I would be in our bedroom upstairs, drawing, or building and demolishing Lego skyscrapers

Mother India Café kitchen, with Kulwant Singe, one of Monir's head chefs until 2013.

in between Corgi car chases, and we'd listen to the roars of laughter from the living room, happy that people were getting along.

In my late teens I got into art school in London, and my friends arranged a send-off party in our favourite Indian restaurant. This was heading towards the end of the 1980s, but food-wise things hadn't changed much in Curry Valley, as Gibson Street in Glasgow's West End was then affectionately known. I thought it was about the tastiest thing on the planet: old-school 'British' Indian fare, but they did it very well. It's hard to beat the beautiful contrast of a chilly night and a warm, inviting room. The aroma would hit you as you walked in, tastebuds gagging for that first mouthful. There was plenty of banter from the waiters, who were usually of Asian descent but as Glaswegian as the rest of us.

My student years in London opened up a wonderfully wide world of food, friends, and one or two girlfriends. We were all skint, even with our part-time and summer jobs, so restaurants were a rare treat, but through careful research I did track down a few cheap and cheerful haunts for special occasions and clumsy, tongue-tied dates, thinking that a bit of sophistication was the order of the day to impress a young woman. More often than not, they weren't very impressed by me, but loved the food. One girl, who I remained friends with, thanked me later for introducing her to a couple of gems where she then took the guy she chucked me for. Always nice to be of service.

What I did do was learn to cook in an endless succession of multi-occupancy flats, and even a squat at one point. I was very lucky to have a talented Thai junior chef as a flatmate for a while, as well as an Italian couple who taught me how to make the most meagre of ingredients into something surprisingly good.

When I graduated and moved back to Glasgow in the early 1990s, my old school friend Scott, who'd been the kingpin of my Curry Valley send-off, told me about a new restaurant called Mother India. It was announced with a kind of civic pride, as if to say, 'Well, you might have been away doing your fancy London stuff, but let me show you what we've got.' So off we trotted and I've never looked back.

I remember being absolutely blown away that first time. We went upstairs to Scott's favourite corner and I found myself in this beautiful Victorian room. It had dark-wood-panelled walls and huge leaded windows, with a random collection of elegantly battered Edwardian tables and chairs. The menu was small, but when the food came it was like nothing I'd ever had in a restaurant before.

Memories flooded back of Sundeep's mum's kitchen, and of Indian and Pakistani friends' home cooking in London and elsewhere, but this had its own edge, its own unique take on things. The meat was on the bone, but off the bone it fell and you could taste the difference. My chicken was so moist, the freshness of the delicately spiced spinach leaf seeping into the meat, but leaving the innate 'chickeniness' intact. Every mouthful was a burst of individual flavours, all working together subtly, but with a deep underlying hit. The slightly grassy flavour of Scott's lamb shone through, enriched rather than drowned out by the sauce, and again, the meat was so tender.

Scott knew I liked my food, but sat with this huge Cheshire-cat grin as I yo-yoed from respectful silence to cries of 'This is amazing, Scott! This is absolutely fantastic!' At one point we were actually in some strange hinterland between laughter and tears at how good the food was.

So this became our place, and by the mid-1990s me and my partner Ann would go regularly with Scott and his partner. Other local friends would join, and whenever Danes came over or Londoners came up, it was the first port of call. Family gatherings would be organised. At one point, Ann and her pal Carol had to organise a big reunion, so to Mother India it was. Our friends were by now all scattered far and wide, so Glasgow may not have seemed like the natural meeting place to Gertrud in Düsseldorf, but once she tasted Monir's food, she knew it made sense.

I was actually sitting round a table in Scandinavia, speaking Danish and eating pickled herring, when my mobile rang and there was Monir. I only answered because I didn't recognise the number and thought there may be something I had to deal with back home.

I was absolutely delighted that Monir was interested in working with me at Mother India. He'd seen some of my work and seemed to like it, and I'd come up in conversation when he was having a meeting with my old pal Ketan, who gave him my number. Ketan — another alumnus from the Cubs and Curry Valley — had become a bit of a legendary waiter on the Indian restaurant scene, and is now a restaurateur himself.

Monir and I hit it off from the word go, and over the years I've seen his new ventures grow and develop from the germ of an idea into places that have become part of the life of two great cities, Glasgow and Edinburgh. The food is so good, and his staff do such an excellent job, it sometimes seems there's nothing much I can add to the mix with my photography and design. But thankfully people seem to have responded well to my small input, so hopefully I've added rather than taken away.

As I have said, my dad was a born-and-bred Glaswegian, and he, Monir and I share a language of irreverent in-jokes and obscure references, which we find hilarious. Like most people, we've had our share of personal sadness, but somehow the daft jokes keep things going, and a laugh, especially round a table with some good food, is a great healer.

Over the years our families have also got to know each other. My daughter Nina is only a little older than Monir's younger son Amaan, and they're very fond of each other. Monir and I are usually very busy, but we always make time for each other personally, and sometimes still join forces work-wise.

I've been very lucky to have had the chance to know and work with some hugely inspirational people from all walks of life, including other great chefs and restaurateurs, and it's always a pleasure when some of these people meet and get along. I became good friends with the chef Pete Begg when I was working on one of the *River Café Cook Books*. He's a Glasgow boy, and when he came up to visit I had to take him to Mother India. Needless to say, he was immediately won over. Years later, when I got to know Monir, I thought it would be great to introduce them. They got on famously straight away, and part of the inspiration behind the inclusion of Monir's special in-pot smoking technique (see page 271) came from a lunch we had together. Pete is now an integral part of Jamie Oliver's team, and knows a thing or two about good food.

Over the years, Mother India has received plaudits from around the world. Monir's story shows how a talented chef from humble beginnings in a Scottish city, with an innate understanding of Punjabi food, can produce recipes of world-class excellence and startling originality. What makes Monir special is his very personal vision, his understanding of produce, balance and flavour.

When Monir and I first sat down and talked about a book on Mother India, one of the things we wanted it to do was reflect two sides of the same coin as to how Indian restaurants fit into our cities. We wanted to let Monir's story give an honest insight into his rough-and-tumble, behind-the-scenes life, and at the same time we wanted the photographs to allow the reader to walk a day in the life of a modern city, with Indian restaurants as an integral part of the cultural and physical landscape.

Above all, we wanted the recipes to reflect Monir's talent in drawing from the roots of the ancient art of Punjabi home cooking with his own extraordinary twist.

I was born and grew up in Glasgow in the 1960s. My earliest memories are from the time my family lived at London Road in the East End.

We lived in a big tenement flat, with four bedrooms and a huge sitting room. It was blackened from a century of ingrained soot, had rattling windows and was in a bad state of repair generally, but we loved it. The block had been built in the 19th century, just around the corner from the old Monteith Row, which in its heyday was a grand Victorian terrace overlooking Glasgow Green. Though you could still see the remains of faded grandeur in some of the buildings, sadly this particular part of the East End had fallen on very hard times, but we needed a large flat as there were quite a few of us to pack in and it was the cheapest place for my dad to buy. We were one big happy family sharing this pile: my biggest brother Jamil and his wife, my brother Bashir, my sister Jamila, my other brother Majeed, my parents and me. My dad and I slept in a wee snug that was tucked behind a curtain off the kitchen. My mum shared one of the smaller bedrooms with Jamila, and the rest were packed into the remaining bedrooms.

At that time most people also had a lodger. Ours, John, was a Glaswegian with a bunnet (a Scottish flat cap) and we became very fond of him. He was only about four and a half feet tall but was a real character who liked a drink. He used to sell the paper – the *Evening Times* – and was one of an army of wee men in bunnets who would shout 'Times' from street corner stalls (though once they'd shouted it out a few hundred times, it was more of a noise than a word, but everyone knew what it meant). I spent a lot of time in his room, just chatting about stuff. John had a good heart and each Friday or Saturday, however much he'd drunk, he always came back with sweets or an ice cream for me or my sister. Like most kids, we had a seriously sweet tooth, so this was a big treat. He wouldn't drink in the house; it was always in pubs, but as our flat was two floors up, if he'd been particularly thirsty I sometimes had to give him a bit of a hand up the stairs.

The post-war East End was still really run down. The buildings were black and crumbling, with gaps in between left after the Luftwaffe bombing raids. Yet in spite of this, there was a great sense of community, and we played happily with all the neighbouring kids. There were local shops: Derek the grocer's, two or three dairies and a few ice-cream parlours. Some of the shops used to have window displays full of sweets and if you could afford to go into the shops with a penny, you could go in and ask for the 'penny tray' and pick your favourite. My sweet tooth meant that I was a visitor as often as the odd penny would allow.

I haven't always been interested in food. In fact, as a child I was a particularly bad eater. I was fussy and there weren't many things I liked, particularly vegetables and lentils, which are what my mum cooked with a lot. Red daal was a staple in our household, accompanied by things we thought were exotic – traditional Glasgow fare of chips and jam butties. One of the few Indian things Mum made that I did like was a chicken and gravy dish served with bread. But if in doubt I'd ask for a bit of bread and butter and if I was lucky the butter got mixed with sugar. When she made vegetable curry, I would say that there was no way I was eating that, so rather than have me not eating at all Mum would sometimes give up the fight and say, 'I'll make you chips'. As in so many Scottish homes, chips made a regular appearance on our plates, particularly mine.

Glasgow was famous, or perhaps infamous, for its tenements. These Victorian four-storey blocks of flats were beautifully built and ranged from tiny 'Single Ends' (one room with an outside toilet for the whole close) to grand flats which had huge rooms and ornate ceilings. At that time no one bothered restoring them, or maybe even knew how to, so many just crumbled. Back then town planning up and down the British Isles was geared towards moving people out of the poorer parts of the inner city into housing estates and high-rise blocks on the outskirts of town. Thankfully many tenements were saved and have since been beautifully restored and they are now considered some of the most desirable places to live.

By the time I was about seven, our flat had become a cosy home; my dad had invested in improving and decorating it and he was proud of the result. It was decided that the tenement next door was dangerous, so they started pulling it down. I remember the cranes and demolition balls– it was all very exciting until one night at 3am there was a knock at the door, and my dad was told that something had gone wrong and our flat was about to fall into a hole in the ground, so we needed to move out right away. We, along with all the other

Gardiner Street in Glasgow's West End looking down to Dumbarton Road and across to the Riverside Museum designed by Zaha Hadid. The beautifully renovated tenements, international students and foreign number plates on the cars are typical of the West End and reflect how much Glasgow has evolved in the last few decades.

families from our block, spent the night in a police station and were then sent to a community hall. Evicted and homeless.

We never received any compensation for our loss. My dad said later that the residents didn't know how to go about it, so they just shrugged their shoulders and moved on. However, we were allocated a council house in Cranhill, a housing estate on the outskirts of town.

The people from our close had all been split up and sent to different council estates. The friends I'd grown up with had been moved to all corners of the city and I remember feeling loneliness for the first time. My brothers and sister were all at secondary school by then and I remember the headmaster saying that I was the first Asian they had ever had in the primary. There hadn't been many Asian families in London Road, but it was a bit of a shock to be the only one in a new school. Of course it happens the world over but some kids were suspicious of me because I was different. I wasn't beaten up but there was a bit of verbal abuse. Many of the kids stood up for me, but others just kept staring. It was difficult to make friends. Even worse, some kids would pretend to be my friend and then they would slag me off later. I tried my best to fit in, eventually being allowed to join in the football with a gang of ten others, but nobody would talk to me. After the match they would all go off into their own little crowd and I would be left on my own again.

One striking memory is of Muhammad Ali being a big star at the time and because my second name was Mohammed, kids used to say, 'Is Muhammad Ali your uncle or something?' I used to reply, 'Aye he is.' He was everyone's boxing hero, so I just blurted it out. I thought it might buy me a bit of respect but of course, as you can imagine, it didn't really work.

Glasgow was famous, or perhaps infamous, for its tenements. These Victorian four-storey blocks of flats were beautifully built but at that time no one bothered restoring them so they just crumbled. It was decided that the tenement next door to ours was dangerous, so they started pulling it down. I remember the cranes and demolition balls – it was all very exciting until one night at 3am there was a knock at the door, and my dad was told that something had gone wrong and our flat was about to fall into a hole in the ground, so we needed to move out right away.

In 1971, Dad decided to leave Cranhill. He was having to travel too far to work, so we moved back to the East End, where Dad bought a tenement flat on Morris Place, just next to our old, now demolished, flat. What a relief. I was so glad to be 'home' and back in the local school

The Lewis's department store was a short walk into town and a city institution. Among many glamorous attractions it had the ultimate food hall and it was amazing to walk around it. I couldn't buy anything as I didn't have money to spend but I still loved to wander in its rooms soaking in the atmosphere. It was built around the same model as Harrods, a grand Victorian food hall with all the stands, the high ceilings and amazing smells. Lewis's was not quite as grand as Harrods but it was a big deal for a fourteen-year-old boy, particularly one with a sweet tooth. The cake stands were incredible: row after row of pastries, tarts and sponges – piled high and just crying out to be scoffed.

In contrast to the luxuries of my afternoons spent in the Lewis's food hall were food and mealtimes at home, where economy was the order of the day. At this time hens were our big thing. My dad had met a farmer called Willy who had lots of hens. In fact, Willy had so many hens laying eggs that every now and then he needed to get rid of some of the less productive ones – the older birds. Willy's hens were cheap and Dad could spot a good deal.

So every Tuesday between three and four o' clock Willy the farmer would arrive in his van to drop off four live hens and an egg box. It was £3 to £4 for four hens – never over £4, but a different price each week. This was a very good price at that time. Hen meat is very different to chicken; chicken is younger and tastier, but at that time it was really pricy and considered a luxury food, so hens were definitely the more economic option.

When I arrived home from school the smell in the hall was terrible, but we had to live with it until Dad got back from work, then the two of us would slaughter the hens. Being Muslim, we had to kill them in a certain way so that the meat was halal – by cutting the hens' necks and letting the blood drain out. Dad used to clean, gut and pluck them and there were our four hens ready for the week. I really didn't look forward to coming home on Tuesday.

My sister and mum weren't involved in the killing as women aren't allowed to do it, but Mum had to transform the slaughtered birds into dinner. Old hens are quite tough and the dark meat does not hold much flavour, so the secret to cooking them it is to create a tasty gravy. Mum would put a whole hen into a pot with plenty of water and cook the vegetables – most probably potatoes, onions and garlic along with it. The ingredients were very basic. In went some spices – Mum was a simple cook and never used more than three or four, so in this case probably just some chillies and turmeric; salt, and the whole thing was then simmered away until the water had reduced and produced an aromatic

Looking west as the sun sets along Dumbarton Road. This photograph as been used as the back cover of the biography of the iconic Glasgow band, The Blue Nile, whose music is said to reflect the sometimes brooding atmosphere of Glasgow's streets on darkening nights.

broth or gravy. That was our hen curry. We would eat it with chapatis, which Mum always made.

I still buy hens today – three or four every week, though not live ones(!) – just to make stock. Hens make a thicker, heavier stock than chickens.

Lewis's was a big deal for a fourteen-year-old boy, particularly one with a sweet tooth. The cake stands were incredible: row after row of pastries, tarts and sponges – piled high and just crying out to be scoffed.

Monir.

*Smeena's (Monir's wife) granny, Salamat
Bibi, with Monir's mum, Hajra Bibi.*

Saturdays were special and we used to have fish and a fruit loaf from the Salt Market. Mum had two ways of cooking the fish so we'd get one or the other every Saturday. It would either be fish and chips in breadcrumbs or fish curry with boiled potatoes.

We're Asian so of course Mum liked to add a touch of spice to the fish's breadcrumb mix, which made it special and one of my favourite meals.

The curry would be a flaky curry. Mum would stir it around so much that all the haddock would break up, which for some reason made the spices get right into the flesh so that it was really, really tasty. All the flakes were covered with a very dry spice. When I make it now, for presentation I try to keep the fish whole if possible – it looks nicer – but I never get the same taste as when it had crumbled.

Mum also made a special dish using tinned salmon. There wasn't a fixed day for this; it was simply a wee treat. Salmon was a very luxurious fish and we couldn't possibly afford it fresh but Dad really loved his tinned salmon. Mum used to make him a dry salmon and egg curry and here I've turned it into a recipe based on her dish using fresh instead of tinned salmon. I named it after her – Hajra Bibi.

Another treat, but more of a guilty pleasure during my teens, was deep-fried pizza from the chip shop. It was the cheapest piece of pizza you can imagine – dough like a cardboard frisbee with some kind of bright red sauce painted on top, a few gratings of rubbery cheese, then into the deep fryer it went. It would be served up with chips and that would be your pizza supper. Gorgeous. It was just me that would eat this fine delicacy; nobody else I knew would touch it. A couple of years ago I tried a slice again. The memories came flooding back, but it's definitely a young man's game; I think you need a cast-iron stomach to survive it at 50 without feeling a bit iffy afterwards.

HAJRA BIBI'S SPECIAL SALMON

Serves 4

¼ teaspoon mustard seeds

½ teaspoon cumin seeds

3 tablespoons vegetable oil
  or light olive oil

1 medium onion, finely
  diced

4 cloves of garlic, finely
  chopped

4 green chillies, finely
  chopped

1 plum tomato, chopped,
  or 2 tablespoons tinned
  chopped tomato

1 teaspoon salt

¼ teaspoon ground
  turmeric

4 eggs

4 salmon fillets (roughly
  15cm or 175g each)

½ teaspoon crushed black
  pepper

a handful of fresh
  coriander, chopped

Over a medium heat, dry-fry the mustard seeds in a large frying pan for about a minute until they start to pop. Add the cumin seeds and then, about 10 seconds later, add 2 tablespoons of vegetable oil. Add the chopped onion and sauté gently over a medium-low heat for about 5 minutes, until soft. Pop in the garlic and green chillies and cook for a further 5 minutes over a medium to low heat. Lastly, add the tomatoes. Turn the heat down low, simmer for 10 minutes, then add the salt and turmeric. If the mixture starts to stick to the bottom of the pan at any point, just add a tablespoon of water to loosen it.

Put a tablespoon of oil into a separate non-stick frying pan and heat until it starts to smoke. Meanwhile boil the eggs for 1 minute, then remove the pan from the heat, cover it, and leave for a further 4 minutes. Put the salmon into the frying pan and sear for about 1 minute on the skin side and 30 seconds on the non-skin side. Remove the fillets from the frying pan and add them to the pan of spiced tomato sauce. Peel the boiled eggs, then halve. Finally add the boiled eggs and simmer over a low heat for 5 minutes, or until the salmon is fully cooked through. It should look opaque and feel firm to the touch.

Season with black pepper, then scatter the coriander on top, cover with a lid and simmer for a final minute or so.

This is delicious served with chapatis. Get stuck in and let this traditional Indian flatbread soak up all the mouth-watering tanginess of the sauce. The two combine perfectly, and the plain, slightly floury taste and bite of the chapati wraps itself around the flavours, bursting on to your tastebuds in a perfect balance of taste and texture.

The dish also works well with potatoes. Cook some small or baby new potatoes for 15–20 minutes, depending on their size, in salted water, leaving the skins on, and toss with a tablespoon of butter. Add a wee handful of chopped coriander or parsley if you fancy.

HADDOCK WITH BABY POTATOES AND CREAMED CABBAGE

Serves 4

25ml sunflower oil

1 medium onion, finely
  chopped

4 cloves of garlic, finely
  chopped

a small knob of ginger,
  finely chopped or grated

4 green chillies, finely
  chopped

1 teaspoon cumin seeds

1 teaspoon fennel seeds

½ a star anise

3 ripe tomatoes, chopped

¼ tablespoon salt

½ teaspoon ground
  turmeric

20g butter

4 haddock fillets
  (approx.170g each),
  skin off

16 baby potatoes, cooked

For the cabbage

1 cabbage, sliced

1 teaspoon mustard seeds

15g butter

½ a medium onion,
  chopped

2 cloves of garlic

1 teaspoon salt

3 tablespoons double cream

black pepper

Heat the oil in a medium pan and add the onion. Cook gently for 1 minute, then add the garlic, ginger and green chillies for a further minute. Keep cooking over a low–medium heat and add the cumin, fennel seeds and star anise. Simmer, stirring, for a few minutes, then add the tomatoes, salt and turmeric and cook for a further 5 minutes. Add the butter, then put in the haddock fillets and cover them with the sauce. Place a lid on the pan and simmer for 5 minutes, or until the fish is opaque and cooked through.

Meanwhile, parboil the cabbage for a couple of minutes. Sprinkle the mustard seeds into a separate pan and place over a medium heat. Once the seeds start to pop, add the butter, onion, garlic and salt. Cook for 2 minutes, stir in the double cream, then add the cabbage and cook for a further minute. I like the cabbage to still have a wee bit of bite, but cook it for a bit longer if you prefer your cabbage softer. Season with black pepper at the end.

Put about 4 of your baby potatoes on to each plate, and put the haddock fillet next to them with a good spoonful of the sauce. Add a generous helping of the cabbage on the side and serve.

M y oldest brother Jamil was quite ambitious. In 1976, despite all my dad's reservations, he wanted to go into business and better himself. So he set up two shops: a newsagent in Livingston and a general grocery store in Deans, which is an older village incorporated in the New Town of Livingston in West Lothian, about three quarters of the way between Glasgow and Edinburgh. It was all hands on deck. Me, my sister and my other brother Bashir had to go down there at weekends and help out. We stacked shelves, served customers, anything we could do to make ourselves useful.

Then one day my brother saw this derelict property in Bathgate, a town a bit further west of Livingston, and he decided that it would make a good restaurant. So Jamil and two partners took the place on and Bashir, who had been talking about packing in his electrical course and coming to work at the restaurant, started working in a kitchen in one of the popular restaurants back in Glasgow so that he could train himself up.

Setting up the restaurant took a long time and it was a stressful period. Through naivety and not understanding restaurants properly, Jamil and his partners underestimated the costs of doing it up. But at that time people often did just jump from running grocery shops to restaurants. They simply thought, 'Well, restaurants are a kind of shop.' And the chat among the Asian community especially was that a restaurant was somehow a step up from a corner shop, with a higher profit margin.

The additional costs put a lot of pressure on the family and the strain on everyone was visible, but I was excited at the idea that there was going to be a restaurant in the family. I was very young and didn't know much about restaurants, so it was interesting to watch all the developments. My brother used to take me down to the site and I would wander around and see the progress.

The day the Taj Mahal opened there was a big party at lunchtime and I remember lots of people working. At one point the chef was organising the staff and one of them asked what I was doing. I was out in the back yard because it was a nice day but I was just hanging around. When I replied that I wasn't really doing anything, he said, 'Do you mind peeling a bag of onions?' Of course I wanted to help out so I got on with it straight away. After I finished the first, he said, 'Can you do another?' I think I peeled seven bags of onions that day, working flat out until four o'clock. I've never peeled so many onions.

What I really liked about helping in the kitchen was working with adults; lots of adults. All day I had chefs and waiters coming up to me saying, 'How you doing; are you all right? How are you? Too much for you?' I was a wee boy and I just loved the attention. When I got hungry they made chips for me and it was the first time I'd ever had frozen, ready-prepared chips. It was a whole new

On the right is Monir's brother Bashir, with their mother, Hajra Bibi, in the centre, and Bashir's wife, Kalsoom.

taste for me. They were all so perfect, cut the same and pure white in colour.

Sadly after the buzz of that day working in the restaurant, I had to go back to helping out in the shop, which I didn't really enjoy so much. But two or three weeks passed and the restaurant got busy. The area had really embraced it because it was the first Indian restaurant in the town. There were chicken and lamb dishes mainly – dhansak and Madras curries and for 30p extra you could have a vindaloo, but European dishes were also being sold as well to keep a balance. Nearly all Indian restaurant menus throughout the 1970s and 80s had a small 'European Choice' section and I remember the infamous chicken Maryland and steaks being popular with non-curry fans.

But Jamil and his partners were struggling to get enough staff and cope with the demand. So Jamil came to me one day and said, 'Why don't you come and work on Friday and Saturday in the restaurant after school? I'll pay you £7 a night, so £14 a week.' I thought that sounded very, very good.

So on Friday afternoons I headed straight from school to Buchanan Street bus station. It was quite a long bus ride out to Bathgate but I enjoyed it. I would work Friday and Saturday nights, stay with Jamil or Bashir's family in Livingstone after my shifts, and then head home to Glasgow on Sunday.

I started at the bottom – washing the dishes and cleaning up – but I liked working with a group of people. And for a young boy, men's conversation was very exciting so I would just watch and listen, fascinated by the rough and ready talk of football, cars and women, with more than a few practical jokes thrown in. Being a KP (kitchen porter) is probably the hardest and least respected job in the whole restaurant but it's really important – a good KP keeps the restaurant ticking and a bad KP can cause a lot of problems. Our restaurant was busy so there was a never-ending cycle of dishes coming in and it could get quite boring at times. But after a while my brother thought he'd give me a bigger challenge so he got me on to salads. I thought that was a big promotion and I was proud that for the first time I was part of the mechanics of what was heading out to the front. All the European dishes had a bit of salad on each plate and the tasks were really basic; I was just chopping lettuce and tomatoes and slicing cucumbers, although those I had to arrange in a fancy design. If things got really busy I would help with the rice and the coffees.

Eventually I was asked to try my hand at being a waiter. I must have been about 15 by this time. Waiters had to wear smart outfits so I got myself all dressed up in a green jacket with a black collar. It was quite nerve-wracking. I didn't get any training so I just had to learn on the job, follow the other waiters and try and copy what they were doing. It was also quite daunting for a shy teenager to be suddenly thrown into dealing with the customers face to face. I never felt I had a natural talent for being a waiter. Even then I knew

Here on the right, on the corner of Battlefield Road and Holmlea Road, is the Alishan Tandoori, which has been open for over 25 years. There has been an Indian restaurant on this site since the 1970s. Legend has it that the first Indian restaurant in Glasgow was opened in 1954 by Sultan Ahmed Ansari, called the Taj Mahal, when 2 shilling (10p) curries were the norm.

that the kitchen was a more natural environment for me. I was doing simple things to begin with – setting tables, clearing dishes and changing the paper tablecloths – but I didn't always enjoy it. One of the main reasons was some of the clientele. Many of the customers were great, especially the early evening ones – really nice local families with whom we got quite friendly. So things were OK up to about 10.30pm, but then the pubs shut and the drinkers came in. That was when I would start getting nervous. Heavy drinkers weren't something I'd experienced before and some of the people there were not very nice at all. I didn't have to serve them luckily but I saw a bit of drunkenness and sometimes anger; it could get pretty rough. It was a problem well known to anyone working in Indian restaurants all over the British Isles at that time. The restaurants were often licensed to serve alcohol till quite late, so some punters would see the 'curry house' as a place to go after 10 pints in the pub; they'd want a few more with their vindaloo. It wasn't much of an incentive for the restaurateur to provide the finest cuisine. There were some clients who actually scared me when they walked through the door – they were very aggressive towards the other staff. We weren't allowed to sell alcohol to take away or serve it while customers were waiting for a carry-out and that sometimes caused an argument. Sometimes they'd run away without paying their bill; often there'd be shouting. And then there were certain kinds of people that just came in looking for trouble.

So the period around the pubs' closing time was a tense time for everybody but it was something that stayed with me; I used to have sleepless nights because it scared me, especially on a Saturday night.

Finally the day came when I was asked to serve tables – just the ice creams and coffee to begin with, but I quickly progressed to taking orders. The only thing I couldn't do was serve alcohol as I was still too young.

While my weekends were spent soaking up restaurant life in Bathgate, back in Glasgow I wasn't exactly focusing on my school work. It didn't help that the culture in our school wasn't so much about studying as about being good at football or just having a carry on. Looking back I feel sorry for the three or four kids who did try to study; everyone else used to slag them off and call them swots. I bet most of them have had the last laugh now. But looking back there simply was no way I could manage part-time work and study. At that time most Asian kids were expected to help out in the family business and Jamil in particular thought I should help the cause. I really admire those kids who balanced their jobs with their academic work. I didn't.

Even though the Taj Mahal was the death knell for my short-lived academic career, I was excited about my weekends at the restaurant. I remember my brother, Bashir, saying, 'Don't get too involved in this. You concentrate on

your studies.' He was already wary that it might not be a good future for me – it might be bad pay and bad conditions. But I was drawn to the buzz of the kitchen and each Friday I looked forward to my time in Bathgate more and more.

There was also the money. Out of the £14 I earned each week, I'd give ten to my mum and kept four for me. The money for Mum went towards the housekeeping.

In 1980, when I was 16, Dad retired and decided he wanted to sell the house in Copeland Place and go away, first to visit Mecca, then back to Pakistan to look after the land he had bought there in the early 1970s. He always used to make comments like, 'I want the house's grains – *ghar ki dana* – I want to eat the house's grains.' At that age, we didn't understand what on earth he was on about but now I get it. Everything we consumed in Scotland was bought in shops and he wanted to go back to the simplicity of living off the land. It was in his bones – he always felt that in his heart he was a farmer and it was his dream to return home and work the land again, growing and making food. And after all those years he realised that he was finally able to return and fulfil this ambition.

I think the plan was for my parents to leave when my sister got married. She got married in 1980, so after the wedding Mum and Dad started packing. Dad said to me, 'You stay here for six months and then come and join us there.' He got my passport ready for me.

I'd never been to Pakistan before, I had never even travelled, so they set me up with a travel companion – a husband and wife who could help me with the journey. Arriving in Faisalabad was a huge culture shock. There were cows walking on the road and horses, donkeys and buffalo just hanging around. Over the next few days there were countless cousins, aunts and uncles to greet, which was strange and exciting at the same time, as this was the first time I'd ever met a family member outside my immediate family. Everyone was so happy to see me; there were big smiles and huge handshakes and I remember feeling overwhelmed by the whole experience. They loved people coming from Britain, though always assumed you must be from London. How's things in London, they would say. 'I don't know. I only passed through it once on the bus on the way to the airport.' These exchanges were all conducted in Punjabi and unfortunately mine wasn't the best. I got by but to this day, my Punjabi comes out with a thick Glaswegian accent, which my family over in Pakistan found highly amusing.

After about three or four days I said to Mum, 'When are we going back to Scotland?' She just smiled gently and said, 'Why don't you stay here with us.' I think that was the first time it really sunk in that my parents weren't coming back. They tried to convince me to live there too: 'You should stay with us, get married and everything is here for you; there's land.' As far as my father was concerned, I was the lucky one, I was young. My other brothers and sister were married and had their own lives but I could stay in Pakistan and be provided for. He kept referring to 'the land'. Land has huge significance for Punjabis so how could I possibly want to go back to Scotland; the only reason to go there was to make money and that was no longer necessary. I'm not sure whether I

Monir's mum, Hajra Bibi.

fully appreciated the significance of what he was saying at the time but as he walked me around his land everything fell into place: the comments over the years, the importance of ownership and family. I could feel his sense of pride as he showed me around the farm; this was where his life had started, with the land that he had worked on for his family. As he was running me through the technicalities of farm work, I wasn't, to be truthful, that interested. I was 17 and frankly I didn't care. Dad spoke at length about what was growing in the fields; what to do with a certain crop; how buffalo are fed, and little did I realise how valuable his words would be to me later on. This was not my home though. My home was in Scotland and I was homesick.

In Pakistan I was introduced to one of my cousins, Soofi. He must have been in his forties, a small man in stature, but very strong, large and loving in his personality. He smiled all the time. The first time I met him, my dad told me that he ran a successful food stall. Soofi was making a good living from his stall, so he decided to open a restaurant in Faisalabad. I'd never met anybody like him — somebody who was so interested in food. He loved feeding people and he loved talking about food. Every 15 minutes he would ask you, 'Would you like this to eat? Would you like to try this?' And when I went to his restaurant I could see how much he was loved and how much his food was loved. It's something that's always stayed with me and has no doubt influenced my own interest in food.

After six months in Pakistan, my health was being affected. The heat was getting to me; I had lost a lot of weight and was practically unrecognisable. It was time to go home and to start to work again. Given my academic record, there were not many options open to me but I knew where I wanted to head. So to the kitchen I returned.

Land has huge significance for Punjabis. As my father walked me around his land everything fell into place: the comments over the years, the importance of ownership and family. His sense of pride as he showed me his heritage was quite moving; this was where his life had started, with the land that he had worked on for his family.

Family and friends gather at Monir's brother Bashir's house, with the always entertaining Nasser Mohammed, on a visit from Edinburgh teasing us 'Weegies about the wonders of his town, while Bashir's grandson Abdullah plays on the floor below.

Even though I'd been homesick for Scotland, life when I returned from Pakistan was lonely and at times quite dispiriting. I went back into full-time employment at the restaurant in Bathgate and lived in a room upstairs. By this time the restaurant was losing money and there was a sense of gloom and doom in the air. I missed my parents and I was stuck out in Bathgate, isolated and alone. Bathgate is pretty much midway between Glasgow and Edinburgh, so on my day off, I had two choices. In Glasgow I used to love soaking up the atmosphere. The town was buzzing. I'd have enough money to get myself a good lunch. Throughout the Seventies and Eighties Indian restaurants were springing up all over Glasgow and a lot of them were getting really good. Lewis's food hall was still a favourite place for me, but now I could afford to go upstairs and eat in the restaurant. This was nearly always followed up by a matinee double bill at one of the big city-centre cinemas. Sometimes I would even stay over in Glasgow at my sister and brother-in-law's house in a beautiful part of the West End. Jamila and Nasser lived with his mother, Auntie Rashida, who was a very close friend of my mother's. Nasser is a tremendous guy. He's become a dear friend as well as a relative. He's always tried to keep me on the right track, and has been a great inspiration to me, both personally and professionally. They were a large, close family but I was always welcomed there with open arms. Antie Rashida's cooking was fabulous and I have fond memories of tucking into her chicken curry around a happy table, which was the centre of their home. It was lovely to be there, but sometimes a bit sad as family meals were something I dearly missed since my parents had left.

*Cousins Deena from Glasgow and
Imman from Birmingham playing together
at Mother India, as the adults eat at the
table behind.*

Auntie Rashida's Chicken Curry

Serves 4

4 tablespoons light olive oil

10g fresh ginger, chopped

3 cloves of fresh garlic, finely
    chopped

2 large onions, finely chopped

1 teaspoon cumin seeds

2 level teaspoons salt

2 large ripe tomatoes, finely
    chopped

2 cloves

1 small cinnamon stick

2 teaspoons ground coriander

¼ teaspoon ground turmeric

1½ teaspoons chilli powder

1½ teaspoons paprika

2 level teaspoons garam
    masala

100ml warm water

500g skinless chicken breast
    fillets, cut into 3cm cubes

2 spring onions, chopped

a small handful of fresh
    coriander leaves

Heat the olive oil in a good-sized pan over a medium heat and add the ginger and garlic. When they begin to sizzle, add the onions, cumin seeds and salt and cook gently for about 10 minutes.

Add the chopped tomatoes and cook, stirring occasionally, for a further 15 minutes, until the onions are soft and slightly brown. Pop in the remaining spices and simmer on a medium heat, stirring occasionally, for 3–4 minutes. Pour in the warm water and cook for a further 3–4 minutes.

Add the chicken, mix well, and simmer for 10–15 minutes. Stir in the chopped spring onions and continue to simmer until the sauce has reduced slightly and the chicken is fully cooked.

Before serving, add the fresh coriander leaves. Serve with basmati rice, chapati or naan.

Days off in Edinburgh were about taking in the sites, but also about eating and going to the cinema. It had, and still has, a glamorous, elegant city centre. Edinburgh was always exciting but very different from going back to Glasgow. My heart always comes back to Glasgow.

Meanwhile, the Taj Mahal was getting quieter and quieter. It was surviving, but Jamil and his partners decided to sell up and they got an offer from a person that wanted to make it into a disco. That's when an idea struck me. Jamil also owned another restaurant in a town just along the road from Bathgate that wasn't doing anything, and I thought that I could take it over and tell everybody in Bathgate that we were moving there. Our customers seemed keen, provided that the food stayed the same.

I was 18, ambitious, full of optimism and naïve. I went into partnership with a chef I knew of and decided that I would do the front of house. I thought I had experience. I thought that if 70 per cent of our customers from Bathgate came we could make it work. But the Taj Mahal closed and of course nobody came. The chef walked out shortly afterwards, and though I kept the restaurant open for a few months more, I couldn't cope. It closed, I lost the few savings I had and I was devastated. I couldn't even cover my debts. It was a really low point in my life.

After the bleak end to my time in Bathgate, I headed back home to Glasgow with a sense of optimism and hope.

The Koh-i-Noor was one of the city's most famous restaurants at that time. It was very, very popular but due to old mining works Glasgow had problems with subsidence on certain streets, and every now and again a building would just fall down – a bit like our first flat. Thankfully, these days engineers have worked out ways of reinforcing the foundations and have solved the problem. The Koh-i-Noor fell famously – the old building simply collapsed into the River Kelvin. A bright spark soon opened a restaurant just around the corner called Koh-i-Toor, which quickly took on the fallen star's business. The Koh-i-Noor owners were furious and began court proceedings to dispute the new name. But the bare facts could not be disputed: Koh-i-Toor has a completely different meaning to Koh-i-Noor (Koh-i-Noor is a diamond, while Koh-i-Toor is the mountain Moses climbed up to receive the Ten Commandments), and though the Koh-i-Noor weren't too pleased, they had to swallow it.

The story was the talk of the town, and being a young ambitious type, I wanted to work there. At that time what I wanted more than anything was to live and work back home in Glasgow so it was even more of a bonus that the restaurant was in the vibrant West End. I managed to get a part-time job, working three days a week as a waiter, and I loved it. Working there also meant that Auntie Rashida and her family were just round the corner, so it was great to be able to pop over and soak up the atmosphere of their happy family.

Things were not going smoothly in the restaurant however. The bright spark who first opened it had sold his share to two brothers – Aman and Salam Khan. They were both great guys and good chefs but sadly their hiring skills didn't match their cooking, and we all had to cope with 'the General'. The food was certainly a big step up in quality from the Indian restaurant fare I was used to. Tandoori dishes were all the rage at that time and the brothers had a real talent for them. They were made in a proper charcoal oven, and we waiters would serve them sizzling hot from their cast iron dish, placing them piece by piece on to the customer's plate. It was mouthwatering stuff which I was proud to serve. But the General had been taken on as the manager and he wasn't exactly what you'd call a people person; kind of the opposite in fact. He had a couple of favourite waiters, but didn't seem to like the rest of us one bit, so we got dog's abuse every single shift. He didn't like customers either, so they didn't fare much better. I remember him standing at the door at 10.45pm, and if somebody arrived, he wouldn't welcome them in, but would often just shout stuff across the room, like 'There are no starters … There will be no teas and coffees after your meal.' As you can imagine, even though the food was good, many customers just didn't come back.

An Asian street performer at Glasgow's West End Festival, one of Scotland's largest cultural events, which celebrates the cultural diversity of the city. Overleaf: Performers representing the French and Chinese communities.

Sunnah Khan, sitting on the banks of the River Kelvin on a little tidal beach under Kelvin Bridge in Glasgow's West End.

I remember spending one shift peeling bag after bag of onions – in the loft for some reason because it was such a tiny kitchen. Afterwards I came down and asked what the staff curry was that night. 'Fish and cabbage' bawled the General. I was horrified. After all that hard work, we were being given fish and cabbage. But when I tasted it I realised how wrong I'd been. I can still recall those flavours. It was an amazing combination of fish, spiced up with cabbage, unlike anything I'd tasted before. The strange thing was, back then, that the staff curries would be much more authentically Indian than the food served to the customers even though that, in its own way, was also delicious, when done well.

I was young, scraping a living together, barely making ends meet and living in a dingy flat where I shared a room, but on my doorstep was all the buzz and excitement of the West End. There were people from all corners of the world there: bohemians, musicians, artists and students. And there was even a small Asian community. I felt comfortable and welcome – I fitted right in.

At the Koh-i-Toor, however, things were going from bad to worse. The brothers had sold it on to a local grocer, who brought in his own chef and the food suffered badly. For some strange reason, he also decided to keep the General on. So the customers who had stayed loyal to the food, despite the abuse they'd been getting from the manager, were now faced with mediocre fare on their plates, and the place got quieter and quieter. One day I came in and the General took me to one side and told me I was about to get the bullet, so I thought I'd better jump before I was pushed. Years later I met the owner at a function and he asked me why I'd left the restaurant. I told him what the General had said to me. And his response was, 'If I was going to sack you, I wouldn't have broadcasted it first.'

I'd heard rumours about a restaurant in the West End called Ashoka that was doing very well so I phoned them up. A few days later I started a part-time job and that was when I met Balbir, a restaurateur who was becoming a bit of a local legend at the time.

I remember the first time I met him, I was introduced and he said, 'Come here, come here.' He fixed the ribbon round my back and tidied me up a wee bit. I watched how he interacted with his customers and I knew that before me was a higher league of person than any I'd worked for previously. Balbir was an educated man, thoughtful and interested in the wider world, as well as being a talented musician. He really cared about the quality of the food and the service and it showed. He was also ahead of the game. Ashoka was offering a different menu to many of the popular curry houses at that time; Balbir liked Goan-influenced dishes, for example, and this was reflected in the emphasis on dishes with coconut and lime coming out the kitchen — that was pretty rare and exotic at that time.

Overleaf: a couple of mine and Monir's favourite folk musicians Eddi Reader and Phil Cunningham enjoying a folk night in Dukes on Old Dumbarton Road, round the corner from Kelvingrove Art Gallery and Museum and Mother India café, Glasgow.

1970s POACHED CHICKEN

This is the way many Indian restaurants cooked in the Seventies. My version below is a pretty healthy way of eating Indian food, as the chicken is poached and the sauce has surprisingly little fat. Not an authentic Indian style of cooking, this is something developed by British Indian restaurants that is still tasty and brings back memories for those of us old enough to remember. When Indian restaurants first opened in the UK they tried to do proper traditional Indian food, but people weren't ready for it. It looked and tasted too rough for their palates and expectations. The meat would probably have been on the bone as well.

The method of cooking a dish such as this poached chicken was a breakthrough, a compromise between Indian food and Western expectations of taste and presentation. During the Sixties many Indian restaurants opened and closed, as the proprietors still hadn't found a balance between the food they would eat at home and the food their customers were prepared to embrace. The Seventies changed that.

Serves 4

1 medium chicken, skin on (approx. 1.5–1.8kg)
3 tablespoons light olive oil
4 tablespoons slow-cooked onions (see page 274)
1 tablespoon garlic purée (see page 273)
1 tablespoon ginger purée (see page 273)
2 green chillies, finely chopped
1 teaspoon roasted cumin seeds (see page 270)
1 small cinnamon stick
1 black cardamom pod
1 x 400g tin of chopped tomatoes
½ teaspoon ground turmeric
1 teaspoon salt
½ teaspoon red chilli powder
1 teaspoon paprika
350ml chicken stock (see page 235)
½ teaspoon garam masala

Fill a very large pan with water and add ½ teaspoon of salt. Bring the water to a simmer. Carefully drop the chicken into the pan and bring back to a gentle simmer (you want to have at least 5cm of water above the chicken). Poach for 30 minutes, then cover with a lid and turn off the heat. Leave the chicken in the pot for a further 30 minutes, then carefully remove it from the pan and set aside to cool.

Heat the oil in a separate pan. Once hot, add the onions and cook for 3 minutes, then add the garlic and ginger purées and the green chilli. Cook for a further 3 minutes, then add the cumin seeds, cinnamon stick and cardamom and simmer for 2 minutes. Add the tinned tomatoes, turmeric, remaining salt, chilli powder and paprika and let everything cook over a low heat for 5 minutes.

When the chicken is completely cool, discard the skin and take the bones out. You want to be left with 2 chicken breasts and 2 leg portions, thighs and drumsticks attached.

Put the chicken into the pan of spiced sauce mixture, add the chicken stock, and simmer for about 3 minutes. Serve sprinkled with the garam masala.

HALIBUT (OR MONKFISH) WITH SPICED CABBAGE

Serves 4

25ml sunflower oil or light
   olive oil
1 medium onion, finely
   chopped
4 cloves of garlic, finely
   chopped
1 small knob of fresh
   ginger, finely chopped or
   grated
2 green chillies, finely
   chopped
1 teaspoon roasted cumin
   seeds (see page 270)
½ teaspoon roasted fennel
   seeds (see page 270)
½ teaspoon roasted
   mustard seeds (see page
   270)
½ a star anise
6 fresh curry leaves
½ x 400g tin of tomatoes
1 teaspoon sea salt
1 teaspoon red chilli
   powder
1 teaspoon ground turmeric
1 small cabbage, sliced and
   parboiled
1 teaspoon olive oil
4 pieces of halibut (or
   monkfish) approx.125g
   each), skin off
1 lime, cut into wedges

Heat the sunflower oil in a medium pan and add the onion. Cook gently for 5 minutes, until translucent and soft, then add the garlic, ginger and green chillies and cook these for a further 3 minutes. Keep cooking over a low to medium heat and add the cumin seeds, fennel seeds, mustard seeds and star anise. Cook, stirring, for a further 2–3 minutes, then add the curry leaves and tinned tomatoes. Simmer for 5 minutes, adding a little water if the sauce starts to stick to the bottom of the pan.

Add the salt, chilli powder and turmeric and simmer for a further 3 minutes, then add the parboiled cabbage and stir well adding a splash of water if the sauce seems dry.

Heat the olive oil in a separate pan. Add the halibut and sear one side for about 2 minutes, then flip it over and cook the other side for a further minute. Remove the fish from the pan and add it to the pan of tomato sauce, placing it on top of the cabbage. Cover with a lid to steam-cook the fish for about 4–5 minutes so it's opaque and cooked all the way through.

Serve warm, with flatbread and the lime on the side.

I returned to Pakistan when I was 21. My parents asked me to come over and my wage from Ashoka enabled me to cobble together the fare. It had been four years since I'd last visited. I went over and stayed a month and then my dad decided to come over to Scotland to sort out a few things so my mum and I had two months by ourselves, looking after the animals – two buffalo and a goat.

Before my father first left Pakistan to come to Scotland he had owned a buffalo, which he sold to pay for his ticket over. I still find it so remarkable that when he went back, he managed to buy a buffalo from the same herd, a great, great, great granddaughter of the original.

Buffalo were vital. The first thing people would say when they came to the house was, 'Is the buffalo giving milk?' If there was no milk, there would be no butter, buttermilk or yoghurt. And if they're gone, how could you cook? What's more, if you melt butter and purify it you get ghee, which was like gold dust. Most farmers would sell their ghee because the price was so high.

How the buffalo were cared for was therefore very important as it affected the quality of their milk. My parents used to feed them a special diet to extract the best-quality milk possible. Mum used to boil cottonseeds. Cottonseed is a popular livestock feed as the hulled seeds are high in protein and when mixed with greenery and other grains provide a nutrient-rich diet. The buffalo loved it and their milk was indeed full of flavour.

Watching the buffalo being milked was mesmerising: the pure white, thick, creamy milk produced was beautiful.

Once they had been milked, Mum used to simmer the milk and the next day we'd churn it by hand to make butter. The butter solids would rise to the top, leaving the buttermilk beneath. This buttermilk is the basis of a traditional lassi. The term 'lassi' is often thrown about in the UK to mean any kind of Indian yoghurt-based drink, generally sweetened and mixed with fruit, but the original version varies by region and in the Punjab a traditional lassi is simply buttermilk mixed with salt – never sugar – and spices. I'd never tasted lassi before and didn't particularly like the look of the thin, pale liquid nor the idea of a salty drink, but the searing subcontinental climate makes you seek refreshment by any means you can and the combination of the chilled milk mixed with salt is surprisingly thirst-quenching. Either way, there was little choice; it was lassi or water and while many people thought lassi was a treat, we couldn't drink the quantity we had. Any left over couldn't be kept as it quickly went off so we'd gift it – neighbours and family would bring dishes and we'd fill them.

Coming back home after a visit to Pakistan was always hard. I felt a strong pull between the desire to be with family, particularly as my parents got older, and my homesickness for Glasgow and my ambition to progress and make something of my life back home and in my own way. When I returned to work at Ashoka, the group was just about to open another restaurant, the Spice of Life, just west of the city centre, and they suggested I transfer and work there. I'm not quite sure why they chose that site – the area was scruffy and a bit derelict, but the worst aspect for me was the hours; we were open from seven in the evening to three o' clock in the morning. The clientele was quite a strange mix.

I hated the hours; they were antisocial and unhealthy and I wanted to leave. Fortunately, it was never busy enough to justify staying open that late and eventually the hours changed. That was when I was made the manager. I'd like to say it was because I had the experience and the expertise but I know that it was simply because they couldn't find anybody else. Still, it gave me a confidence boost I needed and after the change in hours, trade started to pick up. Lunchtimes began to buzz with business from the local offices and the restaurant began to get a bit of a reputation for good food, so the nights got busier too. This renewed confidence got me thinking – perhaps it was time to try something of my own.

A chef friend had introduced me to a friend of his who was selling a restaurant in Dalry, a small town about 22 miles south west of Glasgow. I'd never been to Dalry but really liked the restaurant; the building was a bit run-down, but it had a lot of charm, and in a town where it was the only Indian restaurant I thought it had potential. I managed to get some finances together and went into partnership with a friend. We decided to live in the rooms above the restaurant. Once again, naïvety and ambition seemed to have got the better of me. We hadn't done our homework properly. The lease was not as good a deal as we'd originally thought, and we didn't have enough money to actually open the place properly. We should have listened to more experienced restaurateurs. Balbir's business partner at the time, Charan Gill – a very shrewd businessman who famously went on to develop the large and successful group of Ashoka restaurants – advised me against it, saying we were getting a rotten deal; and he was absolutely right. We started with takeaway food only and into the kitchen I went. We needed to keep it simple and quick – cooking that fitted the trends at the time: kormas, tikkas, dishes the British palate was familiar with and liked. We weren't trying to break any ground in the kitchen or create new dishes. We knew the formula that worked at busy Indian restaurants so that's what we did.

BUFFALO MILK PANEER

Makes 200g

2 x 750ml cartons of
  buffalo milk
juice of 1 lemon

You will need a muslin
  cloth for straining the
  paneer.

Put the buffalo milk into a pan and bring to the boil, whisking
to make sure it doesn't spill over. Once the milk comes to a
rolling boil, turn the heat down to low and simmer for about 20
minutes, until it has reduced by roughly 10 per cent.

Remove the pan from the heat, then add the lemon juice and
start whisking, to curdle the milk. After 10 minutes, strain the
milk through a muslin cloth to separate the curds from the
whey. My method is to tightly wrap the muslin cloth so the curds
sit like a ball in the middle, then suspend the muslin over a sink
(or a large bowl if you want to keep the whey).

After about an hour, or when the excess whey has drained away,
squeeze out as much liquid as possible from the curds and try
to shape them into a square. Now you have paneer. Place it on a
clean work surface (or chopping board) and place a chopping
board on top, followed by something heavy on top of that (I
recommend a medium pan of cold water), to squeeze out the
very last of the whey.

Cut the dried-out paneer into 40g cubes, or smaller if you prefer,
and put it into an airtight container. It should keep in the fridge
for 3–4 days, ready for use in a dish of your choice.

To start with we didn't take any wages from the business then slowly but surely it grew — people came back, we started making money and were eventually able to open a fully-fledged restaurant. And although we could also start drawing a wage, we kept putting the money back into the business — we both wanted to make the place better and better. And two years later, the numbers were still heading in the right direction and we were doing well.

Then the call came. Mum needed a cataract operation in both eyes and my parents needed one of their children to be there. As the only unmarried one in the family I was the obvious candidate.

I confess I wasn't too happy about having to go. The restaurant was coming together nicely and it wasn't the right time for me to leave. But I knew I needed to be there for my parents so I scraped an airfare together and left for the Punjab.

The main reason my parents wanted me to come to Pakistan was not for my mother; it was to look after my father. Mum was going to have to stay in hospital for a week to ten days for the operation and once the cataract was removed she wouldn't be able to do anything. Her vision would be blurred and she would need to stay indoors with her eyes covered. So my job was to cook for my parents. This might sound simple but it turned out to be one of the most important learning curves in my life.

The day would start with breakfast and the first thing I'd have to do was find the wood to be able to heat the stove. The wood might be a kilometre away. The eggs would need to be fetched from the henhouse and even the onions might need to be dug out of the ground. Fresh food wasn't stored so everything had to be gathered as it needed cooking. Breakfast would be something simple like scrambled eggs with onions, tomatoes and a little spice and there would usually be some fresh yoghurt from the buffalo.

Breakfast was the easiest meal, but as soon as it was over I'd immediately have to start thinking about lunch and the other chores that needed doing. There weren't just my parents to think about. The buffalo would also need to be fed so I would have to boil their cottonseeds and prepare their feed as my mother did. Then I'd have to gather anything we needed for lunch. We cooked seasonally so I just had to find out what was in the fields then decide on the meals. Herbs and vegetables would need gathering, and then there was the bread. My father grew his own wheat. He sold around ninety per cent of it, but a proportion was kept back for the house so that it could be turned into flour at the local *chaki* (Punjabi for mill) so we could make bread. The smell of that flour is almost indescribable – it was the earth, the land, and above all the smell of home and home cooking all rolled into one.

Making bread was one of the hardest and most time-consuming things for me. At that time, making chapatis was done by the women in the household and it was a skill they learned when they were young so it was second nature to them. Their talent for creating this wonderfully soft, pliable dough and patting it out to make the light flatbreads by hand is inspiring. I've never had that talent and even with the conveniences of a modern kitchen, I'm not a natural bread-maker – so I found it even harder to work the dough under those conditions. At home I need to use a rolling pin to roll out dough but at the farm there was not even a proper worktop, let alone any tools of that kind. While my mother would make the dough, shape it into balls and go to the stove, where she would take the balls out and shape the chapatis by hand there and then, I needed to go to the house to roll out the balls on a flat surface, then I'd take them out to the stove. The whole process must have taken me at least double the time it took Mum.

The heat really affected me and after lunch I'd need to rest. Then it was up and time to think about dinner. Often I'd make a *daal*. Pulses are a staple in Indian households: they're cheap, easy to prepare and can be kept in the dry store for months without being affected by the heat so you know there will always be a meal to hand. I'd soak my chosen *daal* for about half an hour: *mansoor ki daal, chana daal* or *urid daal* (red lentils, chickpeas or urad lentils), depending on what I felt like, then boil it. I think there's a time in your life when you want your food to be fiery and fierce, but as you get older, you return to wanting more basic flavours and this was certainly the case for my parents. They didn't want any fuss or anything complex. Perhaps it's a sort of comfort in simplicity, you just want the natural taste of each ingredient to come through and I had to respect this. So I would keep the lentils really simple. I'd just melt a bit of butter then fry onions and garlic before stirring in the lentils.

My parents' reaction to everything I prepared was always the same: 'OK,' said Dad, while Mum said nothing. They'd never complain about food, but neither did they show any enthusiasm. Dad certainly didn't mean to cause offence and though I understood this I also took it as a challenge, an incentive to try harder next time to see if I could stir a little bit more enjoyment.

Over the course of the weeks and months I managed to develop a routine and even began to enjoy it all. I was focused and keen to learn – no longer a young boy, shy of speaking or asking questions. I needed to learn and adapt so I had to go into the fields and ask the farmers questions. The experience was the best sort of training I could have had – being forced to study the ancient art of Indian home cooking in its most basic form, from the ground up, learning its core principles.

Cooking for my mum and dad and trying to get them a bit more excited about food continued to be a daily challenge but I loved it. And there were always people popping in to see how I was getting on. I did become the butt of some of the neighbours' jokes – home cooking was a woman's domain – but I laughed them off. I could feel my cooking skills improving and my palate developing; I was cooking for farmers and there was no cheating – you had to spend the least amount of money possible on ingredients so all we bought in were the lentils and salt. For everything else we had to live off the land.

SCRAMBLED EGGS WITH POTATO AND TOMATO

Serves 2

25g butter

1 small onion, finely chopped

1 clove of garlic, crushed

1 small green chilli, chopped

1 teaspoon roasted cumin seeds (see page 270)

1 teaspoon salt

½ teaspoon ground turmeric

2 medium waxy potatoes, cut into 1cm cubes and parboiled

4 oven-cooked tomatoes, chopped (see page 275)

3 free-range eggs, lightly beaten

½ teaspoon black pepper

Put 20g of the butter into a medium frying pan and place over a medium heat. Once the butter is foaming, add the onion, garlic and chilli. Cook for about 2 minutes until nice and soft, making sure to stir with a wooden spoon and keeping an eye on the heat so you don't brown the mixture.

Now add the cumin seeds, salt and turmeric. Let everything cook for a further 2 minutes, then add the diced potatoes. Add the remaining 5g of butter and stir over a low heat until the potatoes are cooked through (you may need to add a splash of water to stop them sticking).

Add the oven-dried tomatoes, along with the eggs, and stir. Cook for 30 seconds, then remove the pan from the heat for a few seconds, returning it to the heat for another 10 seconds. If you like your eggs very soft, stop cooking at this point, but if you prefer a less runny scrambled egg you may want to leave them for a few more seconds on the heat. Gently stir the egg mixture off the heat and add the black pepper.

Serve immediately, with toast.

WHOLEMEAL CHAPATIS

Makes 8–10 chapatis

275ml water

500g wholemeal chapati flour, or plain wholemeal flour, plus extra for sprinkling

½ teaspoon vegetable oil

A tava (see page 268) is best for making chapatis. They are available in most Asian shops at reasonable prices – try to find a heavy-based one. Alternatively you can use a heavy-based griddle pan.

Pour 90ml of the water into a deep bowl. Add all the flour and start mixing with a wooden spoon. Pour in the rest of the water gradually, continuing to mix until all the flour has been incorporated. Cover the bowl and leave to rest for 15 minutes, then wet your hands and give the dough a good knead. Coat the dough with oil and cover the bowl with clingfilm, then put into the fridge for 30 minutes to rest.

Take the dough out of the fridge and divide into roughly 100g balls. Put a tava or griddle on a medium heat until it has really heated up.

Sprinkle some flour on a work surface. Place one of the dough balls on the flour, turning it round until it is fully coated. Press it down with your hand and roll it out into a 20cm circle. Pick up the chapati, dust off any excess flour, and gently place it on your tava or griddle. Turn it over after 20 seconds, then after another 20 seconds turn it over again. Place a clean tea towel over your hand and apply gentle pressure on the chapati until it is cooked on both sides. (If you have a blowtorch, you can use that instead of the tea towel method – this will make life easier.) Make the rest of the chapatis the same way.

URID DAAL

Serves 4

250g urid daal
1 teaspoon ground
    turmeric
1 tablespoon sunflower oil
25g butter
2 small onions, sliced
4 cloves of garlic, finely
    sliced
2 green chillies, finely
    chopped
½ teaspoon roasted cumin
    seeds (see page 270)
1 black cardamom pod
1 small cinnamon stick
3 plum tomatoes, skinned
    and deseeded
1 teaspoon tomato purée
1 teaspoon salt
½ teaspoon red chilli
    powder
a small handful of fresh
    coriander
½ teaspoon garam masala

Wash the urid daal and put it into a pan with 1 litre of water and
½ teaspoon turmeric. Bring to the boil, then reduce to a simmer
for 10–15 minutes. Check that the daal is nice and soft but
retains a little bit of bite.

Heat the oil and butter in a frying pan over a medium heat.
Once hot, add the onions, garlic and green chillies and cook for
about 3 minutes. Take out a tablespoon of the mixture and set
aside for a garnish at the end, then add the cumin seeds, black
cardamom and cinnamon stick.

Simmer for a few minutes, then add the tomatoes, tomato purée,
salt, the remaining turmeric and chilli powder. Cook for a
further 3 minutes, then add to the cooked urid daal and stir
well. Add the coriander and garam masala and simmer for a
final 2 minutes.

Serve with the reserved onion and garlic garnish, along with
chapatis, mint and coriander chutney and salad.

My routine in Pakistan gave me plenty of opportunity for ideas and daydreams. I was cooking but I was also thinking about cooking back home and I used to dream of one day owning a restaurant where the food would be like the food I was preparing there. I even came up with the name – 'Mother India'. 'Mother' because most of us have comforting memories of our mother's food, and India because though my family was in Pakistan, this type of rustic home cooking had existed for countless generations, long before Pakistan had become a separate country in 1948.

I came back to Dalry when my mum was fully recovered with all this buzzing around my head. But while the seeds of the daydream had been sown, I also needed to be realistic. We were running a very traditional British Indian restaurant serving tikka masalas, kormas and vindaloos and there was risk involved in changing things. My partner William was very reluctant to experiment or move away from what we knew. So I returned to life in the restaurant as normal and it continued to survive. But I kept thinking that perhaps we should look for another place back in Glasgow; that way eventually I could run one and William could run the restaurant in Dalry. And about a year later, William and I caught sight of an empty premises on the street where he lived – Argyle Street in the West End. It was a café that had closed down. Intrigued, we arranged a visit and when told the rent would be £70 a week, we signed the lease on the spot, and our very first Mother India café was born.

I remember suggesting to William that we should try something new. The Ashokas were the dominant Indian restaurants in the West End of Glasgow at that time and they did their thing well, so it would be pointless going down the same road. I suggested having a different style of cooking, a much shorter menu with only about seven or eight dishes based on the authentic Indian home cooking that I'd learned out in the Punjab. So that's what we did. Typically we would serve a vegetable curry made with cauliflower, mushrooms and peas; a lamb curry; about four dishes cooked in the Indian-style wok, the *karahi*; and some kind of curry where the chicken would be cooked on the bone. This in itself was pretty revolutionary. Very few people in Glasgow would have had chicken on the bone and not many wanted it either. People thought that having a breast of chicken was the height of sophistication and that meat on the bone was inferior. I remember one woman actually complaining: 'There is a bone in my chicken,' she said, looking horrified, almost as if to say 'what do you call this?' But we persisted and eventually the risks we took paid off.

Amur Kumar Maurya
Head chef at Mother India
Westminster Terrace.

MUTTON SHANKS WITH PEAS AND SLICED POTATOES

Serves 4

3 tablespoons sunflower oil

4 mutton shanks

2 medium onions, finely chopped

6 cloves of garlic, finely chopped

25g ginger, finely chopped

3 fresh chillies, sliced

1 star anise

1 cinnamon stick

4 cloves

8 black peppercorns

1 teaspoon cumin seeds

1 x 400g tin tomatoes

1 level tablespoon salt

1 teaspoon ground turmeric

½ tablespoon red chilli powder

500ml water

3 new medium potatoes, sliced about 2cm thick

130g frozen peas

Heat 1 tablespoon of the oil in a large ovenproof pan. Once the oil is hot, add the mutton shanks and brown them all over for 3 minutes, then remove and set aside.

Heat the rest of the oil in the same pan and add the onions. Cook for 2 minutes, then add the garlic, ginger and chillies and cook for a further 3 minutes. Add the star anise, cinnamon stick, cloves, black peppercorns and cumin seeds and simmer for about 5 minutes, then add the tinned tomatoes, salt, turmeric and chilli powder. Let everything cook for a further 5 minutes, then add the mutton shanks. Mix well, pour in the water and bring to a simmer. Cover the pot and leave it on the heat for 20 minutes.

Meanwhile, preheat the oven to 140°C/gas mark 3. Put the pot into the oven for 1 hour 30 minutes (checking and turning the shanks after an hour). Take out, add the potatoes, and put back into the oven for 20 minutes, uncovered (add a little hot water if required). Take out again, add the peas, and put back into the oven for a final 10 minutes, or until the shanks are fully cooked.

*Speciality Indian and Pakistani grocer's
Spice Garden in Pollockshields in Glasgow,
alongside the excellent Café Zique
restaurant and café on the site of the old
Hargan's dairy in Partick.*

Mango Lassi

This drink is especially delicious and refreshing when fresh mangoes are in season, but a tasty alternative can easily be made using mango pulp from a tin, which is readily available throughout the year in Asian grocery shops.

Serves 4
2 ripe mangoes, or 300ml
    mango pulp
280ml buttermilk
10 ice cubes
300ml milk
2 tablespoons plain yoghurt
2 teaspoons caster sugar

If you're using whole mangoes, remove the skin and the stone.
Put all the ingredients into a blender and mix together for about 2 minutes, until smooth. Serve immediately in a tall glass.

When we first opened, it wasn't busy. We'd have perhaps three or four tables a day, and it was a struggle to keep anything fresh. But I wasn't too worried. Our clientele loved the new tastes and diners were coming back. I also saw customers I recognised from my days working as a waiter; customers who knew their food, and I felt confident that they would spread the word. That kind of thing would keep us ticking over. And we felt a huge sense of pride in not following the rules. It made us individual, it made us brave and there was a great feeling in that. We were daring to be different, and we felt that we were doing it well. A wee bit of luck came our way too. Across the road from us was a shop called 'Adam's Furniture Shop'. The owner John would pop in with things to sell us: tables, chairs, a till — we kitted out the whole place very cheaply thanks to him. Once he came in to announce that he'd been asked to clear the Italian club, just the other side of Kelvingrove Park: 'Why don't you come with me and we'll go and have a look?' he said. 'They want the kitchen out because they're doing the whole place up.' So I went and there was an amazing, full-range kitchen: 12-ring cookers, fryers, racks, shelves, and John just said, '£175. Take whatever you can.'

In 1990 Glasgow was voted European City of Culture. Nearly all the beautiful old sandstone buildings had been cleaned up during the 1980s and the West End in particular was looking great. There was renewed pride in the city and lots of great art and music being produced, with new festivals and events sprouting up all around town. The summer that year was long, hot and sunny and everyone was heading outside.

We were still quiet at the restaurant. We had our loyal regulars and that helped us tick over, but we needed more customers to grow, and sitting indoors eating spicy food on a hot day wasn't exactly everybody's first choice. Then on a particularly quiet day, we made ourselves lassis to cool off and I had this idea. We put up a blackboard outside, with the sign, 'Cool down with a glass of lassi'. I don't think many people knew what a lassi was back then, but there must have been a curiosity in the word because customers started coming through the door. They were too hot so they came in to see if a lassi could help. We served a plain sweet lassi, a mango lassi and even a salty lassi for those who were willing to try it. And the lassis took off. I had the blender going non-stop all day. And people were enjoying them and finding them refreshing, particularly the salty one. So we survived the period of hot weather thanks to our lassis, which gave us cash flow. If it hadn't been for them, it would have been quite a difficult time. I think the fact that we were so small and called a café also helped us. We weren't

Aly Macrea. Folk musician extraordinaire. Monir and I are both music lovers. I've played and performed a bit as well. Monir in particular loves the sound of the traditional Scottish fiddle, as performed by the likes of Aly.

considered a regular Indian restaurant, which was somewhere you would only really go for a slap-up curry. Here, you could pop in for a cup of tea, which for us meant that behind the curries we had these wee rushes on lassis and tea and they kept us bubbling along.

I really liked the area. It had always been quite a mixed area for Glasgow – multicultural and diverse – and our customers reflected that. There were lots of students, musicians and arty bohemians, but we also had doctors, academics, architects and designers. Open-minded people who liked diversity and something interesting and different. And people seemed to be enjoying what we were doing, so I suppose what we were doing clicked with them. It wasn't just the way our food was cooked but the way it was served too. There weren't any fancy table settings, just basic bowls, simple presentation and really, really good food.

The summer was also an important time for me personally as I was due to be married on August 5th and my mum and dad were coming over for the big wedding.

Smeena and I had got engaged the previous September. For the last few years my mum had been keen to see me settled, which was hard to do from Pakistan. She wanted me to get married because she didn't like the fact I was by myself, and I think she felt quite guilty. She was always saying, 'Get married, and at least you'll come home to some cooked food.' But marrying me off proved difficult. Parents weren't exactly queuing up to marry off their daughters to somebody who worked in catering. At that time being a chef was not the trendy profession it's become. People often tried to hide it by saying they were doing a course. If I said that I was doing a course in computing I had more chance.

My friend Sanjay Majhu told me about how when he was growing up his family used to go to Asian parties. Usually there would be at least three or four doctors there and they were always the stars. People would do their best to say hello or talk to them – they were a big attraction. It's funny because over the last number of years, the chef 'thing' has got to a stage where people would be almost as keen to talk to a chef or restaurateur as a doctor. They'd rather say, 'What's your speciality? What do you cook?' But back then, being a chef was not going to impress anybody.

Things got to the stage where I felt constantly rejected and I decided I didn't want to face the humiliation of trying to meet the right girl. I knew I could easily have gone back home and got married to a perfectly nice girl in Pakistan, and I was reaching the stage where I thought that that's eventually what I'd have to do, but I was Glaswegian and that's the culture and environment I'd grown up in. It's a huge part of what I am, so I wanted to meet somebody here who was also Glaswegian.

Smeena.

I remember the day Smeena Ali's parents were first mentioned. I knew some of the Ali family through a combination of work and family connections, but I had thought there was no point asking them. Some friends of my mum and dad's had said that they'd never say yes so we had all rejected the idea of approaching them. But then one Saturday morning Jamila and Nasser knocked on my door. 'Come on, we're going to see a lovely girl,' they said. 'You've only got a slim chance and you have to see her today.' I remember getting butterflies in my stomach but I would never say no to Jamila or Nasser because I knew they always had my best interests at heart, so off we went. By this point I was so low from all the previous rejections that I thought that if it didn't work out this time I wouldn't put myself through the process again. I saw Smeena – or at least I thought I had, but the room was packed out with 20 other people, and I hadn't actually seen her properly. But she'd seen me. So we left and later there was a phone call from Smeena's family – they were quite happy. Smeena wanted to see me again and meet me properly. I admitted that I hadn't really seen Smeena but that I'd really like to. So we arranged another meeting at their house.

When I met Smeena properly for the first time I was very nervous. We've often laughed together about it since. She still giggles, remembering my awkwardness and attempts to impress her. At one point I tried to show off about being just about to buy a Suzuki Jeep, but for some strange reason the thought of being chauffeured around in a small, bumpy, off-road vehicle didn't get her too excited, so we ended up bonding over our mutual love of proper Italian ice cream. Her family owned the Bungalow café in the south side of Glasgow, which they'd bought from an old Italian family, along with Mamma's secret ice cream recipe. Smeena worked there and made the ice cream herself.

The funny thing is that I don't think Smeena's mum and dad were 100 per cent convinced about me, even after my tall tales of Suzuki Jeeps. They had doubts about the security I could offer Smeena as a career in catering has always been more risky than others. Business can be up and down like a yo-yo, and at that time I was still living hand to mouth, with no savings, and in reality Suzuki Jeeps were still a dream. It was Smeena's granny, Salamat Bibi, who put her foot down and said, 'No, this is the boy for you; I can feel it.' She was an amazing lady – full of wisdom, wit and warmth and her family always listened to her. She knew my mum and dad and was very fond of them both. So that was it – a new chapter in my life began; I was engaged.

On Friday August 3rd 1990, two days before my wedding, somebody called me to say, 'Go and buy a *Herald*.'

A critic from the *Glasgow Herald* had visited the café. The paper (now called *The Herald*) was the biggest broadsheet newspaper in Scotland and the critic in question was a man called Raymond Gardner; he was notorious for his opinionated reviews. But he'd given us a fantastic write-up. At that time, a review for a restaurant of our size was an amazing, slightly surprising achievement. To be honest, I hadn't even read one of his reviews before, but I was soon to understand their power because what happened in the next three or four hours was unbelievable – the turnaround, the people coming in. The review he'd written couldn't have been more complimentary, and it showed that he really understood what we were trying to do. From that point on the café was full every lunchtime.

Within hours, our lives changed. One minute we were doing five, six tables a day, and the next we had people queuing up outside. Suddenly everybody wanted to try Mother India and it was very hard to cope with the demand. We somehow managed to get staff – our friends mainly, who would come in to help – but it was hard to keep on top of it all. Not to mention the fact that I was getting married on Sunday. That weekend was crazy. We had visitors coming for the wedding, and we were so busy in the restaurant that I had to be there. I remember finishing at 1am on the Saturday, the day before the wedding. But I was on such a high and the adrenaline just kept me going. The first time your restaurant gets busy, popular even, nothing else matters.

The review was probably the best wedding present I could have been given. I had always had in mind the thought that I wanted to be financially settled before I got married so the timing of the review was perfect. At the wedding people kept saying, 'I saw your review, it was fantastic'; even the doctors, dentists and accountants were impressed.

So, we got married on the Sunday, and by Wednesday I was back to work. It was just too busy to take any time off. It was an important time to consolidate and control how many people were coming through the door so that you don't have this great review and nobody there two weeks later.

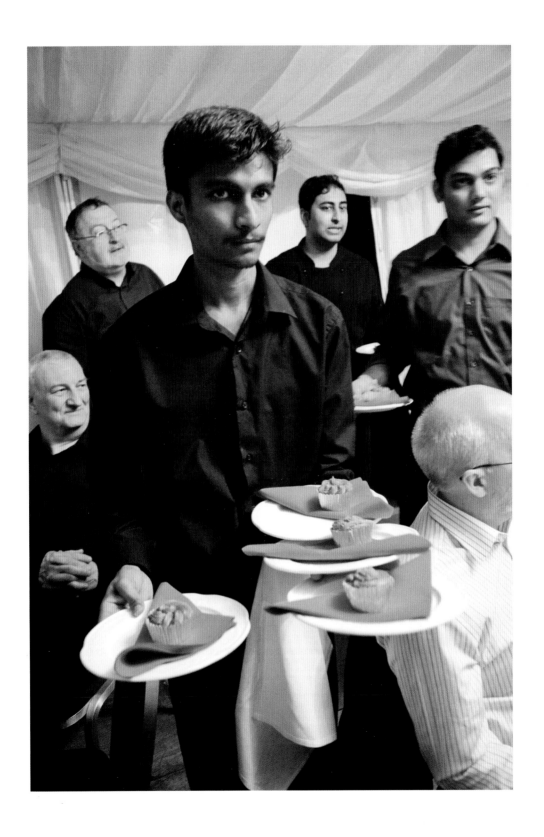

Glasgow was constantly changing throughout that year and there were visible improvements not just to its appearance but to the quality of life there. Things were going really well at the café too, but then one day we had a call from the environmental health planning board. The ventilation system was not up to the job and we couldn't see a way to fix it. The council told us we weren't allowed to operate our cookers with this ventilation system so we could either switch to using microwaves (reheating was allowed), upgrade our ventilation system and move it so that it was directed up the building, which was impossible because we were at the front of the building and didn't have access to the back wall. The people who have the site now dug down and built a kitchen in the basement with the correct ventilation. But we didn't know what to do, and didn't have the money for anything major anyway. So we took the really tough decision of closing down. It was a very, very big blow for us.

To have to close was heart-breaking but we had no option so we decided to cut our losses and look for another place. Luckily, the bank was quite willing to help us. They'd seen that we had been doing well and the accounts were looking good so they said they'd agree to fund another place if we found one. Unfortunately that took six months.

We couldn't get a place in the West End as nothing was really coming up in our very limited price range, but we saw this place under the railway arches, on the south side of the River Clyde, literally under the railway tracks heading into Glasgow's central station.

It took a long time to get the lease sorted. The railway company owned the property as it was under their tracks but their surveyors dragged their feet. It took them six months to get the lease organised, and all the while our money was drying up. But eventually, having borrowed quite a bit of money to pay for everything, the premises were ours. We put in the kitchen and some furniture – we still had some furniture from our old place – and got the restaurant open. The site had been a pub before us and we just kept a lot of the décor, as it hadn't been that long since the place was done up.

The first few days were terrible. I'd thought that we would open, put a couple of adverts in the paper announcing the reopening of 'Mother India' and people would remember us and come. I'd imagined that we would get at least half our previous customers and everything would be OK. On the Friday we opened, we had a few guests come in, perhaps two or three tables, but that Saturday was probably the longest night of my life – not a single table.

The place was much bigger and had much better facilities than we'd had on Argyle Street but I'd really underestimated a few things. For our old customers, coming to that area was too much out of their zone; they just didn't associate it with going for a night out. I hadn't realised the importance of a restaurant's connection to the area around it. The whole culture of the West End area was villagey – geared to going out locally, or maybe into nearby parts of the city centre. There weren't so many people living around this new place and there was no sense of buzz or excitement to draw them.

There was the odd loyal customer that did come over, but everyone said that the atmosphere just wasn't the same as in the original Mother India café. It was a big open space and it didn't feel as close and comfortable. We'd lost that cosy quirky café feeling. In restaurants, there's a strange kind of x-factor, a sensation people have that being there just feels right. The food is only a part of eating out: customers also want good service and they want to feel comfortable. It's the whole package. With the first Mother India café, we'd concentrated on the food and the rest just fell into place. The food was just as good here. In fact it was exactly the same menu, but in this new location things were tougher. We'd gone from being a small place with 25 to 30 covers and people who were willing to share tables, to a bigger, far less characterful place with 70 to 80 covers. Maybe the pub décor put people off, maybe it all felt too modern, or maybe the location really was the main problem, but either way we hadn't re-created that magic x-factor of the first café. It was a hard lesson learned.

Things were a struggle at the beginning. We were in this big space with just two of us working – me in the kitchen and one waiter – and it was like starting all over again. But eventually we started getting about three or four tables each day. We'd lost our West End clientele but we were building things up a wee bit with a loyal crowd, some of whom were coming up from the south side of the city and going back to spread the word.

Yet another problem we had at that time was that Dalry was going downhill. Perhaps our biggest mistake was that because the first Mother India had proved so successful, we decided to take the same menu to Dalry. We thought it could only improve things, but in fact it was a big mistake. We were trying to take a formula that was working very well in Glasgow's West End, to a village in Ayrshire. People didn't like the food. They didn't like the fact that we didn't make multi-coloured rice, or bright red tikka masalas. It was all too earthy for them – too basic. They thought they were being short-changed by it not being the same as before. One lady, who had been a regular customer, came in and said, 'I want the proper authentic stuff.' People had an idea of what a curry was – even though it had not an awful lot to do with the food you would eat on the Indian subcontinent – and that's what they wanted. More than anything that woman was saying, why have you changed? She was comfortable with what she'd been getting before. And she was right, we probably shouldn't have changed. So we tried to go back to the old menu, but this just made it look like we didn't know what we were doing.

Unfortunately for us, this was the last roll of the dice and we were being threatened with bankruptcy. The bank wasn't happy because what they had seen happen in the first Mother India café certainly wasn't happening here. We couldn't pay back our loans on time, so the interest rates got higher and higher. All our bills were getting further and further into arrears. It was awful. When you're trying your best to make something work, money worries like that can make you despair. After about a year of struggling, we hoped we'd soon see signs of things turning round, but for the bank we'd reached the point of no return. Eventually the plug was pulled — our debts were too high and we went to the bank and closed everything, including Dalry, down.

Karam.

My son Karam was born in 1992. It was not how I'd imagined bringing a child into the world. I was in financial ruin and things were desperate. It took many months of further misery, and debts piling higher and higher, before I was finally declared bankrupt.

I gave the bank a call one afternoon, just to check the balance and make sure the latest set of cheques we'd written to our suppliers weren't bouncing. My bank manager came on the phone and there was a worrying tone in his voice. He told me that my account had been frozen and I was insolvent. He was sorry, but there was nothing he could do. It was over.

Smeena and I were both very upset but she told me to go and see a friend of her father's who might be able to help me. We quickly grabbed Karam and jumped in the car and went to go and see Michael. I remember being in a panic. The sense of complete failure when you become bankrupt is earth-shattering. Yet it was also tinged with a sense of relief as well: constant money worries are exhausting.

The 15-minute drive to Michael's house felt like the longest of my life. But we talked things through and he agreed to put up some money to acquire the lease for a property. I had caught sight of some premises on Westminster Terrace as I had been driving by one day; it was a fantastic site in the West End, just around the corner from the first Mother India café and I'd known straight away that it would be the ideal place to start something again. At that point, I hadn't yet been made bankrupt, but business was going so badly that I knew a move back to the West End would be impossible financially. Nevertheless I had put in a call to find out who the property belonged to and they had put me through to the owner. After talking for a few moments I recognised his voice – it was Mike Shrigley. I knew Mike from my days working in Spice of Life as he used to be the landlord there, so I was confident about calling him now. If anyone was going to give me a chance it was him. Mike had a good sense when it came to choosing his tenants; he would not necessarily give a place to the highest bidder, but to the person who would make a location work, and amazingly he decided to give me a chance with Westminster Terrace. With Michael's help we got it on a very short lease and we started to get a restaurant set up. Unfortunately, that would take a while and in the meantime I would have nothing to do.

I was not working for the first time since I'd left school and I was getting very down. The only good thing to come out of it was that it gave me time to spend with Karam.

Mother India, Westminster Terrace,
Kelvingrove.

In the summer of 1993 we managed to open Mother India with a single cooker, a tandoor oven and a fryer. Bankruptcy means that you aren't allowed to own or run a business for a minimum of three years after you're made insolvent so I could only be an employee. I was the head chef and it was up to me to make the restaurant work, but having gone from owning and running restaurants to being an employee again was dejecting. Even so, I was glad to get back to work and for the first time in a long time I was actually earning a wage.

The day we opened it was just me in the kitchen and the best kitchen porter I've ever worked with. Bill was a pensioner, so he just helped out on a few nights. He had been a prisoner of war. He was a real gentleman and very hard working. On a quiet night I used to love listening to his stories. He would also chop onions, peel garlic, and keep washing pots till they sparkled.

Shortly afterwards, my sister-in-law Kalsoom came in as a chef. She was an excellent cook. Smeena would also be a big help out front, serving tables and making the customers feel welcome. I was also lucky that in Dalry we had trained a few young people on the old government Youth Training Scheme intended to get unemployed young people into a job, and slowly they came to help me in my new kitchen.

It was clear from the start that Westminster Terrace would work much better than our failed location under the railway tracks. Slowly we were attracting our former West End customers and trade was picking up. Still, it was quite tricky working with Michael and adapting to his ways. He wasn't really a restaurant man, and didn't see things the way I did. I learned a lot from him about the business side of things but he didn't understand the subtleties of running a dining space. Our costs were too high, he kept telling me. However, things managed to tick along and in 1995 Smeena and I decided we could take our first holiday together as a family – two weeks under the Florida sun.

Our holiday was coming to an end when Smeena suddenly became very dehydrated and started hallucinating. She didn't know where she was or who she was. It was extremely frightening. After a few days of sedation and rehydration we managed to get her on to the plane back to Glasgow and called our GP as soon as we got home. He tried giving her sleeping pills, thinking she was still dehydrated and tired, but after a couple of days there were no signs of improvement and in fact she started getting worse. She wasn't sleeping at all apart from the odd half an hour and had absolutely no energy. She was becoming more and more delirious, having strange and worrying hallucinations. Finally she was taken to hospital where she was diagnosed with a severe mental breakdown and bipolar disorder. She was very ill and slipping away from us, deeper and deeper into her depression.

It was a very difficult time for everyone. Karam was only three years old.

He was lost without his mother and didn't understand what was going on. I had to look after him, as well as visit Smeena and look after the restaurant. I was lucky our families rallied round otherwise it would have been impossible to make things work. I finished work at the restaurant, then had to pick up Karam from my mother-in-law's house at around 11pm. He would be asleep and we wouldn't want to wake him so sometimes the two of us would just sleep there. Going to visit Smeena was even harder; she was still deteriorating. I was exhausted, lonely and sad, desperately worried that Smeena would never make a recovery. And on top of this I kept thinking that the restaurant was about to fail again. It was becoming stale – Michael's cost-cutting exercises were reducing the quality too much and things were sliding.

And just as I thought things couldn't get any worse, I had a call from my mother saying that my father was very unwell and that one of us needed to come over. I was in no position to go and my mother understood this, but my brothers Bashir and Majeed quickly made arrangements to go to Pakistan. They were lucky. They got there in time.

SPICED HADDOCK AND TOMATO

Serves 4

1 tablespoon sunflower oil
1 tablespoon yoghurt
juice of ½ a lemon
¼ teaspoon salt
¼ teaspoon roasted cumin
  seeds (see page 270)
½ teaspoon roasted fennel
  seeds
4 green chillies, crushed or
  finely chopped
1 level tablespoon tikka
  paste
10–12 oven-cooked tomatoes
  (see page 275)
a small knob of fresh
  ginger, cut into thin
  matchsticks
4 haddock fillets

Put the oil, yoghurt and lemon juice into a medium to large bowl and whisk together. Add the salt, spices, green chillies, tikka paste and roasted tomatoes and keep stirring until you have an evenly textured marinade. Stir in the fresh ginger.

Dip each haddock fillet into the marinade and turn so that each piece is well coated. Put the fillets on a baking tray and set aside for 30 minutes.

Preheat the oven to 190°C/gas mark 6 and roast for 12 minutes, or until the fish is cooked through (the timing will depend on the size of the fillets).

MURGH PALAU

Serves 4

40ml sunflower oil or light
  olive oil
1 whole medium/large
  chicken, cut into 8 pieces
  (skin removed, but keep
  the bones in)
1 small onion, finely sliced
3 cinnamon sticks
25 black peppercorns
4 black cardamom pods
12 cloves
3 green chillies, finely
  sliced
½ tablespoon cumin seeds
4 cloves garlic, crushed
¾ x 400g tin of chopped
  tomatoes
¼ tablespoon red chilli
  powder
¾ tablespoon salt
1 litre chicken stock (see
  page 235) or water
400g rice

To sear the chicken pieces, add a tablespoon of oil to a large
pan and add the chicken pieces. Let them brown all over, being
careful to not let them stick. This should take about 5–6 minutes.
Remove them from the pan on to a plate.

Heat 25ml sunflower oil in a medium pan and add the onion.
Cook gently for 1 minute, then add the cinnamon sticks,
peppercorns, cardamoms, cloves and green chillies. Cook for
5 minutes, until the onions are golden, then add the cumin
seeds. Cook, stirring, for a further 2 minutes, then add 100ml of
hot water. Add the garlic and cook for 5 minutes, then add the
tinned tomatoes, chilli powder and salt.

Cook for 5 more minutes, stirring occasionally, until the sauce
thickens, then add the seared chicken pieces. Stir well, cover
the pan with a lid, turn the heat to low, and cook for 15 minutes.
Pour in the chicken stock or water, bring to the boil and add
the rice. Start with a medium heat, but gently lower it every
5 minutes so the mixture doesn't stick to the bottom of the pan
(you need less heat as the rice absorbs more water). After about
15 minutes the liquid should have been absorbed, and the rice
should be 90 per cent cooked.

Preheat the oven to 150°C/gas mark 2, then cover the pan with
tin foil and cook in the oven for a further 15 minutes, by which
time the rice should be completely cooked.

Serve with kebabs and raita.

CHICKEN WITH SPINACH LEAF

Serves 4

40ml sunflower oil or light olive oil

4 chicken breasts, on the bone

1 medium onion, finely chopped

3 cloves of garlic, finely chopped or crushed

1 small knob of fresh ginger

3 green chillies, finely chopped

½ tablespoon roasted cumin seeds (see page 270)

4 black peppercorns

2 cloves

1 small cinnamon stick

8 ripe plum tomatoes, skins removed, chopped

100 ml water

½ teaspoon sea salt

¼ teaspoon red chilli powder

½ teaspoon ground turmeric

50g butter

1 packet of baby spinach leaves

a pinch of freshly grated nutmeg

First, sear your chicken breasts. In a large pan over a medium heat, add a tablespoon of the oil and add the chicken breasts. Let them brown all over, being careful to not let them stick. This should take about 5–6 minutes. Remove them to a plate.

Heat the rest of the oil in a medium pan and add the onion. Cook gently for 5 minutes, until translucent and soft, then add the garlic, ginger and green chillies. Keep cooking this over a low–medium heat and add the cumin, peppercorns, cloves and cinnamon stick. Simmer, stirring, for a few minutes, then add the tomatoes, water, salt, chilli powder and turmeric. Add the chicken breasts, making sure they are covered by the sauce, then place a lid on the pan and simmer on a low heat for 10 minutes, before turning the chicken over and cooking for a further 10 minutes, or until the chicken is cooked, adding a little water if the mixture starts to stick to the bottom of the pan.

Remove the lid after 10 minutes and add the butter, then cook for a further 10 minutes. Stir in the spinach, sprinkle with freshly grated nutmeg and simmer for a final 2 minutes.

Serve with basmati rice and/or chapatis.

Eddie was a devout Christian. He was a teacher from Sudan who was working part-time in Mother India while qualifying to be able to teach in Scotland. I liked Eddie and we became quite friendly. After one busy Saturday night I told him I would give him a lift home. He lived in Drumchapel, which is a few miles to the north-west of the West End, and it was late. I explained that I'd have to pick Karam up from my mother-in-law's house first, so it was about 1am by the time we were driving towards Drumchapel with Karam asleep in the back. Eddie started asking me how things were with Smeena and I told him she was really not very well, that she was lying in hospital with no sign of recovery, and that my father was seriously ill in Pakistan, unconscious and about to die. In a soft voice, Eddie told me that he believed that sometimes spirits meet each other when they're both in a hinterland. Perhaps my father's spirit leaving his body would give power to Smeena's. There was something strangely comforting in those words of hope.

It was early evening and I had just been to the hospital to visit Smeena. For the first time in a long time she'd come alive a bit and they said she was showing the initial signs of recovery. Something told me that I should phone Pakistan to see how my dad was doing. My cousin picked up and the first thing she said was, 'Are you alone?' I knew he had passed away.

I have always wondered if there really was a connection between my father's death and Smeena's recovery, that my dad gave her strength as his spirit passed, because Smeena did start to get better – her medication was finally working. We had so much to be grateful for. I realised how lucky we were to be in Britain, to be able to benefit from all the advances in medical science and an organisation such as the NHS. It felt like my father had blessed me as he passed away.

Things were finally starting to look up after what had possibly been the worst period in my life. And although I had the sadness of losing my father, he had passed away at a good old age so I had something to be thankful for.

I almost felt like my father left his luck to me because it definitely changed after his death. I was coming out of my statutory period of insolvency so I was able to own again. I came to a deal with Michael and he left the restaurant, leaving me with complete control of Mother India.

The atmosphere changed overnight. I was amazed at how fast things started to click into place and how much my newfound confidence helped me. I was doing the right things, changing things at the restaurant, and it was all having a positive effect. We were now using the big room upstairs every night. This beautiful room was one of the main reasons I fell for the building in the first place. It's a beautiful wood-panelled room, with a great history. Radio Clyde was born on the ground floor and upstairs used to be a tearoom, so the building had a lot of memories for many people. We used to get quite a few older folk coming in with their children to show them. We've made the odd tweak here and there over the years, but at the start we didn't have to do much at all except tidy it up a bit.

As the restaurant picked up, I made the choice to bring in better crockery and cutlery and most importantly, to change the menu. I didn't have to ask anybody. There was finally nobody to say, 'Oh no, nobody is going to like that', 'that will never catch on', or 'it's too dear'. I could do what I wanted.

In fact I was having a bit of a creative flourish food-wise. I felt a huge sense of freedom and this helped stir my imagination. I started inventing dishes that were inspired by so many of my experiences, a lot of them from my time in the Punjab. I also started to really develop my own style of cooking and experiment more.

Similarly, as strange as it sounds now, the fact that we used different cuts of meats was pretty ground-breaking. Like in the first Mother India café, I served chicken on the bone to keep its moisture and flavour, and instead of cooking with cubes of ready-diced lamb, we'd cook a whole leg and chop it ourselves, or use lamb chops and ribs. What's more, we told our customers what we were cooking – we named the cuts as part of the dish on the menu. Some of these dishes have now become 'classics' for us – much loved favourites that have been on the menu unchanged for years. And that's not because we don't want to change – it's simply that I know how much uproar there would be if I tried to remove them.

BUTTER CHICKEN

Serves 4

30g ghee (clarified butter)

1 medium onion, finely
chopped

3 green chillies, finely
chopped

2 cloves of garlic, finely
chopped

1 knob of fresh ginger,
chopped

6 cloves

5 green cardamom pods

½ teaspoon roasted cumin
seeds (see page 270),
crushed

½ x 400g tin of tomatoes

½ tablespoon tomato purée

1 tablespoon yoghurt

1 teaspoon salt

½ teaspoon red chilli
powder

½ teaspoon ground
turmeric

1 tablespoon sunflower oil

4 chicken supremes
(chicken breasts with the
wing portion still
attached)

300ml double cream, plus
a little extra to finish

20 whole almonds, shell
off

Salt and black pepper

Heat the ghee in a pan large enough for the chicken to fit into and add the onion. Cook gently for 5 minutes, until translucent and soft, then add the green chillies, garlic and ginger. Keep cooking over a low–medium heat for a further 5 minutes, then add the cloves, cardamoms and cumin seeds. Stir thoroughly and cook for another 5 minutes, then add the tinned tomatoes and tomato purée.

In a separate small dish, put the tablespoon of yoghurt, and beat with a small whisk for a moment to remove the lumps.

After another 5 minutes add the salt, chilli powder, turmeric and yoghurt to the sauce. Cook for another 3–5 minutes, adding a little water if the mixture starts to stick to the bottom of the pan.

Preheat the oven to 190°C/gas mark 6.

Heat a non-stick frying pan and add the oil. Once it's hot, add the chicken and sear until the outside is golden brown, then season with salt and black pepper. Add the chicken to the pan of sauce and cook for 10 minutes, then stir in the cream and cook for a further 5 minutes. Decant everything on to a roasting tray or ovenproof dish and scatter with the almonds. Place in the oven and roast for 12 minutes, or until the juices from the chicken run clear.

Serve with plain basmati rice, with a splash of double cream over the almonds.

SMOKED LAMB CHOPS WITH BROCCOLI AND RED CHILLI

Serves 4

3 tablespoons sunflower oil
    or light olive oil
1 medium onion, finely
    chopped
4 cloves of garlic, chopped
25g fresh ginger, grated
4 green chillies, finely
    chopped
1 teaspoon cumin seeds
3 black peppercorns
4 cloves
1 small piece of mace
1 small cinnamon stick
1 black cardamom pod
¾ x 400g tin of tomatoes
½ tablespoon salt
¼ tablespoon ground
    turmeric
¼ tablespoon red chilli
    powder
1kg lamb chops
1 tablespoon olive oil
6–8 broccoli spears,
    parboiled for 1 minute
salt and pepper
2 fresh red chillies, finely
    sliced

For smoking

2 small pieces of charcoal
    (each about the size of a
    walnut)
4 cloves
1 teaspoon ghee, sunflower
    oil or light olive oil

Heat the oil in a large pan and cook the onion gently for 5–10 minutes. Add the garlic, ginger and green chillies and cook for a further 5 minutes. Now stir in all the whole spices and cook for 3 minutes, until you can smell the fragrance being released. Pour in the tinned tomatoes and cook for 10 minutes more, then add the salt, turmeric and chilli powder and cook for another 5 minutes.

Add the lamb chops and mix well. Put a lid on top of the pan and cook over a low heat for 40 minutes, checking every 10–15 minutes and giving the mixture a wee stir. Add a splash of hot water to loosen things up, if anything feels like it's starting to stick.

For the smoking (see page 271), you will have to light the small pieces of charcoal. There are a couple of ways to do this. If you have a barbecue, put the charcoal in and light it using your preferred method. You can also use a blowtorch, or simply place the charcoal above the flame on a gas hob in an old metal sieve, or on a piece of mesh (be careful of sparks). When the charcoal is turning white, put it into a small metal dish. If you don't have a suitable dish to hand, you can improvise one using an aluminium takeaway container.

Take your pan of sauce and chops off the heat and make a small trough inside so that your smoking device can sit in the middle of the mixture, without falling over. Carefully place the cloves on top of the charcoal and pour on the ghee or oil. You will immediately see smoke belting out from your metal smoking dish. Quickly put the lid back on the pan and leave for 5 minutes. This is a surprisingly effective method for infusing the dish with a delicious aromatic smokiness. After 5 minutes, carefully remove the smoking dish from the lamb and discard once cool.

To cook the broccoli, put the olive oil into a non-stick pan and heat until smoking hot. Add the broccoli spears and sear briefly, then season with salt and pepper and finally add the slivers of red chilli. Place the broccoli on top of the lamb chops in the pan and replace the lid.

Serve with wholemeal chapatis and/or plain basmati rice. A finely chopped tomato, red onion and radish salad would also go well with this, adding a nice fresh crispy crunch to the whole experience.

LAMB MUSSALUM WITH LADY FINGERS

Serves 4

25g butter

4 tablespoons sunflower oil

2 medium onions, finely chopped

6 cloves of garlic, finely chopped

large knob ginger, finely chopped

3 green chillies, finely chopped

1 teaspoon roasted cumin seeds (see page 270)

1 medium cinnamon stick

4 cloves

6 black peppercorns

1 blade of mace

1 x 400g tin of chopped tomatoes

½ tablespoon salt

1 teaspoon ground turmeric

1 teaspoon red chilli powder

700g lamb leg, boned and cut into 6cm chunks

a few lamb bones, for extra flavour

1 small bunch of fresh coriander, leaves picked

24 lady fingers (okra)

salt and black pepper

Heat the butter and 2 tablespoons of the oil in a large pan. Once hot, add the onions and cook gently for 3 minutes, then add the garlic, ginger, and green chillies. Cook for a further 3 minutes, then add the cumin seeds, cinnamon stick, cloves, peppercorns and mace. Let everything simmer for a few minutes, then add the tomatoes, salt, turmeric and chilli powder. Cook for another 5 minutes, then add the lamb, along with the bones, and cook over a low to medium heat for about 50 minutes, or until the lamb is nice and tender. You may need to add a little water to stop the mixture sticking to the bottom of the pan. Finally add the coriander leaves.

Heat the remaining 2 tablespoons of oil in a separate sauté pan. Once hot, add the lady fingers and fry for about 2 minutes, stirring all the time and making sure they are cooked through. Season with salt and black pepper, then place on top of the lamb.

Serve with rice or chapatis, raita and a salad.

Previously: Smeena at one of her favourite cinemas, the Glasgow Film Theatre, and Jim Connelly, Monir's friend and partner in the Wee Curry Shop on Ashton Lane in Glasgow's West End. Jim retired in 2012.

Taste was of course my main priority. I wanted to make sure that I stayed true to the principles I'd learned in the Punjab – to extract as much flavour out of every single ingredient and to respect the ingredients I was working with. And instead of serving typical Indian restaurant dishes, such as korma, we created our own versions. Kormas are often favoured among diners because they are considered the 'mild' option on a menu in an array of hot dishes. The spicing is gentle and the creamy sauce is comforting and easy on the palate. We wanted to offer our customers a similar option, and so our Butter Chicken was born. The rich buttery sauce, gently flavoured with cardamom and cloves, is aromatic and fragrant, and the natural flavour of the chicken can still come through it.

What was surprising was how many people at the start would come in and say, 'Give us a korma,' without even tasting anything else. Sometimes, diners might give me a call before they came. They'd say, 'We want to come back but one of our guests can't take spicy food.' That was OK; I would simply make them something without the spice. And often that would lead to a new creation.

Another thing we added later on were vegetable dishes that weren't spiced, just plain carrots, potatoes, broccoli or Brussels sprouts. Again, it was completely against what people were used to, or the idea they had of an Indian restaurant, but they loved it – that spiciness paired with the unadulterated flavour of the vegetable works because spices can clash. If you're cooking a lovely spiced leg of lamb, you want beautifully roasted potatoes with it, not over-flavoured, over-spiced potatoes; there's enough flavour in the lamb.

Many chefs get home after a long day standing over the stove and sit down to beans on toast; they've simply had enough of cooking by that point and dreaming up new dishes for their family and friends isn't a top priority. But things in my home have always been slightly different.

Smeena has never really been into home cooking. To be fair, when we first got married she was working six days a week in her parents' café, so making fancy food at home was the last thing she wanted to do. I remember our first Sunday dinner together. I was sat there, rubbing my hands with anticipation, expecting a meal lovingly prepared by my beautiful new wife, when a plate of chips and tinned sweetcorn was put down in front of me. I had been imagining something like a roast chicken would appear, but Smeena said, 'There you go.' I said, 'Right, is that it?' And it was.

So although my cooking doesn't end when I get home, making the family meals or entertaining friends has always given me an opportunity and an outlet to experiment. Thus in a strange kind of way, Smeena's lack of enthusiasm for the stove has been a blessing. Every now and then though, Smeena has a burst of inspiration. One of these moments came when she wanted to make a particularly healthy but tasty chicken dish. She used a technique she remembered from her mum's home cooking, where the onions are slow-cooked in oil for hours until they're soft, sweet and caramelised, then stored in a container with all their cooking juices so that they can mature and deepen in flavour. Smeena then takes the onions out and uses them as a base for the dish. They provide stacks of flavour and enough moisture for her to build the dish without adding lots of fat – just spices and vegetables. It's another favourite from our menu and amazingly tasty.

Towards the end of the 1990s we were enjoying a period of stability at the restaurant but I knew how quickly things can change so I decided we needed a back-up in case things did go wrong at Mother India. I was told about a place on Buccleuch Street in the city centre. It was a tiny place, there was only enough space for 22 covers, but I liked the area and the rent was low so I decided there and then to take it. The property's owner was a real foodie and a fan of Mother India, so he was happy to lease it to me. He had run a Japanese restaurant there and had spent a lot of money on the place. It was amazing how he had managed to fit a kitchen and a restaurant into such a small space.

At first I chose to make it into a vegetarian restaurant called The Lady Finger. The idea was a bit of fun – I decided to have a chef who would cook and serve so that we would have very few overheads. We tried this for six months but it was pretty slow. It was a nice idea but it wasn't working. So I spoke to my good friend and fellow restaurateur Alan Mawn about calling it the 'Wee Curry Shop' instead and he liked the name. So we turned it into the Wee Curry Shop

and introduced meat dishes as well as a good vegetarian selection. I'd had the
idea that the atmosphere would be similar to the original Mother India café in
the West End — familiar and friendly. I'd loved that place. Nothing had given me
more pleasure than that moment in 1990 when we had that *Herald* review. And
luckily, the idea to do the same made the difference and the Wee Curry Shop
picked up. Later we got the chance to replicate the idea in Ashton Lane, a tiny
wee backstreet in the West End.

SMEENA'S SLOW CHICKEN CURRY

Serves 4

500ml water
3 green chillies
2 medium onions, finely
  chopped
1 ripe tomato, chopped
1 tablespoon light olive oil
5 garlic cloves, crushed
½ tablespoon grated ginger
1 small cinnamon stick
½ tablespoon roasted
  cumin seeds, lightly
  crushed
½ tablespoon black
  peppercorns
½ x 400g tin of tomatoes
¾ tablespoon salt
½ tablespoon turmeric
1 tablespoon red chilli
  powder
1 medium–sized chicken,
  about 1.5kg, cut into 8–10
  pieces, skin off
Handful fresh coriander,
  chopped

Fill a medium pan with 500ml water and add the whole green chillies, onions and fresh tomato. Simmer for 45 minutes on a medium heat, then add the oil, garlic and ginger and cook for 2 minutes. Add the cinnamon stick, cumin seeds and black peppercorns and cook for a further 2 minutes. Add the tinned tomatoes, salt, turmeric and chilli powder and cook for 5 minutes before adding the chicken pieces. Make sure that the chicken is completely coated in sauce and cover the pan with a lid. Leave to simmer for 35-40 minutes, or until the chicken is completely cooked, making sure to give the curry a stir every 10 minutes or so.

Add the chopped coriander just before you take the pan off the heat, stir in and serve with rice, breads and salads.

The Kelvingrove Art Gallery and Museum which houses one of the world's greatest civic art collections. It's the most visited art gallery and museum in the UK outside London, and is opposite Mother India's Café.

By 1998, I was starting to formulate the idea of doing something else with Mother India – opening another venue. A restaurant across the street from Kelvingrove Art Gallery had just closed. I had eaten there a couple of times and had seen its potential. Sadly it got sold to somebody else before I could express an interest but the restaurateur didn't manage to make things work and six months later it was up for sale again so I bought it. People said I was mad. There was a double yellow line right outside the site and the art gallery, one of Scotland's biggest attractions, was closed for refurbishment for two to three years. There was too much stacked against it. After various unsuccessful ventures it had become what is known in the trade as a failed location. But we went for it. I had liked it and lost it but it had become available again, so I felt it was the right time for me now. Things were falling into place.

With this site I wanted to do something slightly different to Mother India and the Wee Curry Shops but I wanted to stay true to their principles. So I had the idea of doing a tapas-style restaurant. It was 1998 and I don't think anybody had had the idea of serving Indian food in small portions at that time, certainly not in Scotland. But I really wanted to get back to the casual-style dining experience of the original café and, most importantly, get everybody enjoying lots of tastes.

The idea of smaller portions or tapas suits Indian food because there are so many different flavours in the food that one dish is quite limiting. And particularly in British Indian restaurants, one dish is often huge – much more than you need. It's much nicer to have two or three plates to try different things. That is of course fine in Indian restaurants when you're in a group of six people or so, but if you're by yourself or in a couple, it's a problem. So the tapas thing conquered all. Tapas are smaller and all come at once so you don't have a chance to have a huge starter and fill up before your main course arrives. You can order more bits and bobs as they come. If you feel you've not had enough, you can order a couple of extra bits.

When we opened Mother India's Café we weren't expecting much to happen. We thought we'd take over, then the art gallery would re-open and things would slowly happen for us. We were expecting to 'bed in', pass our time for a year and a half or so, just paying our overheads before we really got going. But as soon as the doors opened, the idea caught on really fast and we couldn't actually keep up with the demand. We had to take the decision to say, 'It's not a typical restaurant, it's a café-tapas bar' and adjust the way we ran it accordingly. We decided it wasn't a place where our customers would necessarily sit for two hours. We wanted people to have their food, enjoy it and go home after a casual but delicious meal. It was very reasonably priced so that's why we decided not to take bookings. Restaurants need to be booked so that you can sit down and have a long relaxing meal, but here the style was different; a café should be a café – casual. The first come, first served policy was probably the best decision we made, as trying to take bookings would have been really tricky to operate given the fast turnaround on tables. It also helped Mother India in Westminster Terrace. People might enjoy a meal at the café but then want to know that they could be guaranteed a table the following week so they'd book at Mother India.

CHILLI GARLIC CHICKEN

This is one of the most popular dishes in Mother India, where we usually serve it with chapatis and basmati rice.

Serves 4

700g chicken, boned, skin off and cut into 2.5cm pieces
2 tablespoons sunflower oil
20g butter
2 small onions, finely chopped
2 cloves of garlic, chopped
20g fresh ginger, chopped
2 green chillies, finely diced
1 teaspoon cumin seeds
4 cloves, slightly crushed
1 black cardamom pod
1 small cinnamon stick
½ x 400g tin of chopped tomatoes
1 teaspoon salt
½ teaspoon ground turmeric
½ teaspoon red chilli powder
a handful of fresh coriander
a pinch of grated nutmeg

For the marinade

1 tablespoon mustard oil or extra virgin olive oil
1 tablespoon vinegar
1 tablespoon garlic pickle (see page 276)
1 teaspoon salt
2 green chillies, finely chopped
½ teaspoon cracked black pepper

Put all the marinade ingredients into a bowl and mix well. Add the chicken pieces and make sure they are completely coated. Cover and leave in the fridge for at least a couple of hours, and preferably overnight.

Heat the oil and butter in a large pan. Once hot, add the onions and cook gently for a few minutes, then add the garlic, ginger and green chillies. Cook for a further 3 minutes, then add the cumin, cloves, black cardamom and cinnamon stick and let the spices simmer away for a few minutes.

Add the tinned tomatoes, salt, turmeric and chilli powder. Stir well, let everything cook for 5–10 minutes, then add the marinated chicken. Mix well and cook for about 5 minutes, or until the chicken is cooked through, then add the coriander and a pinch of freshly grated nutmeg. Cover with a lid, simmer for 1 minute, then serve.

CHANA DAAL WITH SCALLOPS

Serves 2

100g chana daal (split
    yellow gram lentils)
1 teaspoon salt
¾ teaspoon red chilli
    powder
½ teaspoon ground
    turmeric
1 tablespoon sunflower oil
1 medium onion, sliced
3 cloves of garlic, sliced
1 green chilli, sliced
    lengthways
15g butter
½ teaspoon cumin seeds
4 cloves
1 small cinnamon stick
¼ x 400g tin of tomatoes
a few leaves of fresh
    coriander
½ teaspoon black
    peppercorns, crushed
2 tablespoons light olive oil
6 scallops, without their
    shells or coral

Soak the chana daal in lukewarm water for 1 hour. Drain, then put the daal into a medium saucepan and add 600ml cold water. Bring to the boil, skimming off any froth that gathers on the surface, then add the salt, chilli powder and turmeric, reduce the heat and simmer for 25 minutes, or until the chana daal is cooked through.

Heat the sunflower oil in a pan and add the onion. Cook gently for 5–10 minutes, then add the garlic, green chilli and butter. After another 3 minutes remove about a quarter of the onion mixture and reserve this for garnish. Add the cumin, cloves and cinnamon stick to the pan and stir thoroughly. Cook for 2 minutes, then add the tinned tomatoes. Cook for a further 2 minutes, then add the contents of this pan to the pan of daal. Cook, stirring, for a final 10 minutes (or until the lentils are soft to the touch), then add the coriander leaves and season with the black pepper.

Meanwhile, heat the olive oil in a separate pan. When it sizzles, add the scallops one at a time, searing them for 30 seconds on one side and 20 seconds on the other. Serve the seared scallops with the daal and garnish with the reserved onion. Accompany with chapatis.

HALIBUT AND PUY LENTILS

Serves 4

125g puy lentils (soaked for 20 minutes)
1 tablespoon sunflower oil
25g butter
1 small onion, finely chopped
½ teaspoon cumin seeds, roasted
¼ teaspoon fennel seeds (roasted)
3 cloves garlic, finely chopped
20g ginger, cut into batons
2 fresh green chillies, finely diced
½ 400g tin chopped tomatoes
1 teaspoon salt
¼ teaspoon turmeric
½ teaspoon red chilli powder
Handful fresh coriander
1 tablespoon olive oil
4 medium size prime halibut fillets – about 160gms each
Juice of a fresh lemon
1 teaspoon cracked black pepper

Simmer the puy lentils in a small pan for about 4 to 5 minutes until just tender. Remove from the heat and rinse in cold water

In a large frying pan add the oil and butter, and once hot add the onion. Cook for about 2 minutes then add the cumin seeds, fennel seeds, garlic, ginger and the green chillies. Cook for a further 5 minutes then add the tinned tomatoes, salt, turmeric and the red chilli powder and cook for about 10 minutes. Add a splash of hot water if the pan is sticking.

Now add the lentils and coriander and mix well. Leave to simmer on a very low heat.

In a separate non-stick pan, heat 1 tablespoon of olive oil. Once the oil is hot, add your halibut fillets, pan fry one side for 3 minutes, slightly season with salt, then flip to other side for one minute. Once your halibut is seared, carefully transfer it to the pan with the puy lentils. Add the lemon juice and the black pepper, cover and let it simmer for a minute until the halibut is fully cooked.

*Previous pages, left to right: David
Wong, proprietor of one of Scotland's
best Chinese restaurants, Ho Wong. Andy
Cummings, head chef at the famous Art
Deco Rogano, central Glasgow. Mini Joti,
much loved health visitor who worked in
Glasgow for so many years. Guy Cowan,
of Guy's Restaurant. The Corrigan
brothers, suppliers of fish to Mother India
and the Mother India Cafés. Haji, the
butcher. Colin Clydesdale of the legendary
Ubiquitous Chip, Stravaigin and the
Hanoi Bike Shop. Maqsood, proprietor
of Asian and Continental Grocers and
Butchers.*

The atmosphere inside the café and the look and the feel of the place was and still is very quirky. It feels like somewhere you can just pop in and grab a quick bite, but it also feels very cosy, relaxed and personal. It's got unique character and the front tables have a view across the road to the Kelvingrove Park and Art Gallery. Martin Gray produced a folio of beautiful black and white photographic prints, which he designed to hang, gallery-style, from wires coming down from picture rails around the room. Martin had a very successful solo photography exhibition at the Kelvingrove Art Gallery a few years previously, as part of the Barras People project. It was undertaken with the television producer Fiona White looking at the last of the old East End traders, right round the corner from where I grew up. Martin has a very human and individual way of treating his subject, but above all lets their personality come out. In the Café are pictures of Glasgow which reflect the atmosphere of the city, but there are also pictures of chefs, waiters, waitresses and suppliers of great local produce. There are food heroes, both mine and Martin's, some of them mutual friends of ours: Andy Cummings, head chef at Rogano; Colin Clydesdale, a fantastic chef and owner of legendary Scottish restaurant, The Ubiquitous Chip, as well as the brilliant Stravaigin and Hanoi Bike Shop; and finally Allan Mawn, a great restaurateur, host and big personality. Tragically Allan died very prematurely in 2011, but he always found it very amusing to be on our wall of fame. Most of them are restaurant regulars and it's always a pleasure to see them. They're important to us on a personal level and although many of them are probably a mystery to some diners, anyone who knows Glasgow really well knows who they are and what they represent. The pictures also work simply as great photographs that capture something about the city we are part of.

The art deco dark green tiles on the walls are a replica of the shape used in the Paris Metro, as well as being a nod to the tiled wally closes and Victorian and Edwardian fireplaces in the old Glasgow tenements. The same green is also quite a significant colour in Asian cultures, which links the two histories. The golden flock wallpaper on one of the walls is a nod to memories of Indian restaurants of old.

It's a quirky mix of stuff, but it works and people react very well to it. My brother-in-law Asif is the general manager, and now also an area manager for all our restaurants, and all his staff help him to create a warm and friendly atmosphere, while being fast and efficient. We've had a lot of great staff over the years in the restaurants. Some of them are quite young and some of them have been with us for years. We often get waiters and waitresses who start as university students. We've had people from all over the British Isles, as well as from other parts of Europe, India and beyond; I've lost count of the

nationalities we've had. It's a wonderful reflection of the lively mix of cultures that make up Glasgow. We've also got waiters who have been part of the Glasgow Indian restaurant scene for decades: well-known faces who can share familiar memories with some of our customers, who bring their children and grandchildren in for a meal. Making a restaurant work well takes good food, but all of these other things are an important part of the experience. Everyone wants to feel comfortable and genuinely welcome in a space they like being in. I sometimes feel guilty that our no-bookings policy means that customers are often queuing to get a table, but the queue moves quite fast and thankfully everyone seems to enjoy themselves once they're sitting comfortably and choosing from the menu.

Previous page: Staff at Mother India's Café, Glasgow. Vijay Nayes, much admired waiter and manager on the Glasgow Indian restaurant scene since the 1970s.

Despite being a Glasgow boy through and through I've always loved Edinburgh and had long dreamed of taking Mother India there. I'd tried a venture in Edinburgh not long after the Wee Curry Shops had opened but as things had not really worked out it was always sad to go back to the city knowing I'd failed.

I knew it would be a risk trying again but by early 2008 it was a risk I was willing to take. I knew that I had to get the concept exactly right, but for some reason I felt confident that if I could manage to get the food to the same level as the quality we'd achieved at Mother India's Café in Glasgow and make the place as comfortable and interesting an environment, then the tapas experience would suit Edinburgh.

I looked at a few locations and a premises on Infirmary Street was the one I liked. I'd been there a few times while it was still trading as Baraka, a lounge bar and Middle Eastern restaurant. The location was on a side street but it had a certain charm and it was next to a famous folk-music pub called The Royal Oak. We decided to take it over.

Martin seemed the ideal person for getting involved in the décor again to make his artwork an integral part of the look and feel of the café. We both agreed that it would be very interesting for the interior in Edinburgh to reflect the city and its people, including the Asian side.

I wanted to make sure I built up a good team of staff to get the kitchen and the front of house right. Asif, the manager at Mother India's Café in Glasgow, and Kulwant, our talented head chef, had made such a success of our first café, that I asked them to help me get Edinburgh up and running. My sister Jamila also agreed to help organise things on a local level, which was great. She and Nasser settled in Edinburgh years ago, bringing up their family as locals. There has been plenty of friendly rivalry between them and our 'Weegie' side of the family.

Yet again the site here had had several failures before us so I knew we had to do something quite special to make sure a Mother India's Café would work and be successful. Martin produced a wonderful portfolio of images. He had worked out a way to cover the walls with his work using different sizes and shapes in a way that covered most of the interior and gave the restaurant a sense of belonging to the area around it.

When we first opened I was in the kitchen with Kulwant, getting him and the other chefs settled. It was a huge relief to see that Edinburgh seemed to respond very well to the café. The tapas style of eating proved popular and people seemed to really like the food and the general feel of the place. Customers responded well to the artwork and quite a few asked if they could buy prints of Martin's work, though he resisted. And as I'd learned, it's always helpful

Sudden Snow on Calton Road, Edinburgh. Edinburgh's topography alone is quite extraordinary. On certain summer days it almost feels like something imagined by Walt Disney. Many visitors gaze in awe at these fairy-tale charms, and during the world famous festival everything bursts into life as it fills to overflowing with a global community of arts lovers. But every city has to be lived in, and Edinburgh's residents live out their daily lives through rain and shine, just as people would anywhere else. Here is also a darker beauty, steeped in history. A reminder of the struggles of countless generations of ordinary people, bracing themselves against the elements on cold winter nights.

to get some good press coverage and we were lucky to receive it. We also won Best Newcomer in Scotland's *The List* magazine and Best Indian Restaurant in Scotland and soon we were attracting regulars and tourists alike.

I am still so grateful that things have worked out in Edinburgh and though I still live in Glasgow, I love to go to Edinburgh as much as possible. I bought a flat there, just off the Royal Mile, so that me and my family can enjoy overnight stays. Martin and I have also had some great days out there. We went to accept an award in Edinburgh a few years ago, which was rather a grand affair in the National Museum of Art, and we made a day of it, walking around the city, trying out little cafés and delis, having a spot of lunch. Martin makes me look at things in a new way. He's always looking at how things work together and sometimes sees something and stops to photograph it. He explains what he's trying to do, and why it fits with a project.

And the Edinburgh Festival is without question the highlight of my year; it's incredible to see so many people from all over the world in one city. Edinburgh is a happy city and I always feel like I am on holiday when I go there, even though it's only 44 miles away.

Soon after we'd got Edinburgh successfully underway, we bought a delicatessen back in the Glasgow area. We found a great site at Bearsden Cross, about four or five miles north-west of the city centre. The old part of Bearsden is very charming, with ancient trees and Victorian sandstone buildings. There was a small site available on a side street right in the centre of the shopping hub. We'd put a deli counter in Mother India at Westminster Terrace back when we first opened, but as the restaurant got busier we'd made the decision to remove it and use the space for more tables but we'd always felt that it was a good idea and that perhaps in the future we could have an independent deli.

The Bearsden site was surrounded by other food shops and restaurants so it was the ideal place to try out the deli idea with chilled ready-prepared foods and store cupboard ingredients. The main idea was that people could buy cold food and heat it up themselves at home.

I'll admit that of course it was also good PR for the restaurants in the West End and Edinburgh as well. We would make samples so that people could have a taste and perhaps be inspired to visit one of the restaurants. It was also a place where I could experiment with dishes, try out new ingredients and put them on as specials to see how they were received. Occasionally we would even do cookery demonstrations there.

In 2010, the site next door to Mother India's Café in Glasgow became available to let, with full planning permission for a food premises. The landlord wanted us to take it but I was in two minds. I knew the shop well; it used to belong to a friend of mine called Joe who was an antiques dealer. Joe had been a customer at the original Mother India site in 1990. He was a real character. I remember he liked his food spicy, then after his meal he always needed a napkin to pat the sweat off his head. Joe was always full of good advice and tips. Sometimes he would say, 'Monir, I want you to come to the shop tomorrow. I want you to buy something. Ignore the price, I know you will like it.' I often used to pop over to see him. You had to ring the bell to get in. He used to sit in the back room (where the Den kitchen is now) with his espresso machine and play the violin. As long as he sold a few items a week he was content.

So we eventually took the premises and decided to make it into another deli but this time with a small seating area of 24. In August we opened Dining In and the Den. It was my hope that this new venture would ease some of the pressure on the other restaurants as customers would have another outlet through which to access our food. Dining In, the deli section, offers cooked and chilled, ready-to-cook food, while the Den is the dining area. I was really glad that Mother India was able to provide a lot of different experiences for people, but I knew we needed to clarify things, so Martin and another friend Mark

Previously: my good friend Jerry Whyte sitting in Mother India's Café, Edinburgh, on one of his many visits north of the border from his home in London. Jerry and I go back to my Art School days and we have a lot of shared interests, though my love of food isn't exactly one of them. Thankfully, even he enjoyed the experience of his first meal in Mother India.
A chef on his break round the corner from Mother India's Café, Edinburgh Old Town.
Opposite: Edinburgh Old Town.

McLeish did a great job designing and printing a lovely brochure that anyone could pick up, which illustrated things clearly and beautifully.

As the Den is next door to the café, we did not want to do the same food so we created an alternative menu, which has a lot more fish dishes than at our other restaurants. I've become increasingly interested in fish. We are so lucky in Scotland to have such an amazing natural resource on our doorstep and I wanted to make use of it. So I started introducing fresher, lighter dishes with Scottish prawns, trout and halibut. I used fillets and whole fish and kept the dishes delicate and defined – the dish was built from this wonderful ingredient and championed its natural flavour, unlike the fish curries of many Indian restaurants where the fish is buried under a mountain of spice and thick sauce until it is completely unrecognisable. It's quite hard not to let Indian spices overwhelm some fish species as their flavour is already so subtle and delicate, but if you do it right and work sensitively, seeing which fish is enhanced in which way, the results can be delicious. Particular favourites of mine are halibut and monkfish. They are both meaty fish that can soak up other flavours while retaining a subtle taste and texture of their own.

We kept the design clean and simple, with a big counter for the deli area and a white-tiled seating area dominated by one of Martin's photographs, which shows a typical Caucasian mannequin, dressed in Asian clothes, standing by a window reflecting typical Glasgow tenements. The overall effect is strangely beautiful. I know this was Martin's intent, but I don't know how many customers work out the link between the three elements and us. But most of them seem to love it, especially children, who get transfixed, trying to work out if the mannequin is a real person.

People like the feel of the place and for some the deli counter has added to the atmosphere. By the time we opened we had lots of regular customers and they knew what to expect from us, but this was a different thing again. To start with, some people did not recognise or want to try the selection of food on offer. It was not what they were used to. Some would even walk out, or go next door to queue outside the Café. But we stuck with the menu. It took a few months to get some customers to try it, but now it has a great reputation of its own. It's Smeena's favourite restaurant and she loves to work there at weekends. And now that it has its own band of followers, some of them even say they keep it a secret as it's only small and you generally need to book.

SPICED MONKFISH WITH PAN-FRIED GREENS

Serves 2

For the monkfish

2 teaspoons coriander
  seeds
1 teaspoon cumin seeds
½ teaspoon fenugreek
  seeds
1 teaspoon black
  peppercorns
2 monkfish fillets (around
  100g each)
2 tablespoons vegetable oil,
  for frying
½ lime, halved

For the greens

200g seasonal mixed
  greens (such as spinach,
  cabbage, asparagus,
  mustard leaves, cress,
  leeks)
1 tablespoon butter
2 cloves of garlic, peeled
  and finely chopped/
  crushed
2 dried chillies, crushed
juice of ½ a lemon
salt and black pepper

Preheat the oven to 200°C/gas mark 7.

Spread the coriander, cumin and fenugreek seeds on a baking
tray and toast in the oven for 2–3 minutes, or until the spices
release their aroma. Remove from the oven, leaving it turned
on, and add the peppercorns. Leave the spices to cool, then grind
them in a pestle and mortar or a spice grinder until very fine.
Rub the monkfish fillets with the spice mixture and season with
salt. Set aside for the moment while you prepare the greens.

Bring a large pan of water to the boil and briefly blanch
the greens, then plunge them into a bowl or pan of very cold
water. Drain any excess liquid from the greens and chop them.
Heat the butter in a large frying pan, then add the garlic and
dried chillies and fry for 2 minutes, or until fragrant. Add the
blanched greens and toss together. Season with the lemon juice,
salt and pepper and toss again.

In an ovenproof pan, heat the oil until sizzling. Add the
monkfish fillets and sear all over, then put into the oven and
roast for 6 minutes, until cooked through. Serve hot, on top of the
spiced greens and a wedge of lime.

KING PRAWNS WITH DILL AND GINGER

Serves 4

1 tablespoon sunflower oil
  or light olive oil
20g butter
1 medium onion, finely
  chopped
4 green chillies, finely
  chopped
2 cloves of garlic, finely
  chopped
½ teaspoon roasted cumin
  seeds (see page 270)
½ teaspoon roasted fennel
  seeds (see page 270)
2 cloves, crushed
small bunch of fresh dill
1 teaspoon salt
½ teaspoon ground
  turmeric
24 raw king prawns, shell
  off and deveined
20g fresh ginger, julienned
  (cut into matchsticks)
8 oven-roasted tomatoes
10 cracked black
  peppercorns

Heat the oil and butter in a large pan. Once hot, add the onion and cook gently for 5–10 minutes, then add the green chillies and garlic and cook for about 2 minutes. Add the cumin seeds, fennel seeds, cloves and dill and cook for a further 2 minutes, then add the salt and turmeric. Mix everything together, then add the king prawns and the ginger.

Stir-fry the prawns for a minute, then stir in the tomatoes, adding a little water if it seems dry. Sprinkle with the black pepper, then cover with a lid and simmer for a further minute, or until the prawns are cooked through. They should go opaque and pale pinkish white in colour.

Serve with chapatis or plain basmati rice and salads.

*Previous page: The Dining-in deli counters
in Argyle Street, West End and Bearsden
Cross, Glasgow.*

The idea that Mother India has been open since 1996, and that we now have four other outlets thriving alongside it, is pretty remarkable. I feel I have been very fortunate. It's been a bumpy ride and I've learned the hard way.

When I joined the Indian restaurant scene in the 1970s and 80s, a lot of Indian restaurants were doing similar things as each other, creating a style of Indian cooking that was anglicised and not always that authentic. Along with a handful of other chefs and restaurateurs, I wanted to break away from the norm and introduce a style of Indian dining that had greater ties to its roots in the Punjab. And in this respect, I have been very lucky. The experience of going back to the Punjab and having to learn to cook the core principles of Indian food is not one that many chefs can speak of. Not many of my contemporaries had that piece of luck. Also the chance to learn came at a time in my life when I was young, impressionable and ambitious, and that experience really shaped the course of my career. When I was there, it made me want to bring Punjabi cuisine – the 'real' Punjabi cuisine – home to Glasgow and I have stuck to that principle all the way through, despite sometimes it being advised that it was not a good idea. Today, as always, the menus at all our Mother India outlets reflect this authenticity. It is something that will never change.

But it's not just about the food. When I was creating Mother India, it was as much about opening a restaurant that would fit into the life and culture of a city as its Punjabi roots. I am Glaswegian through and through, and intensely proud of my home, and I wanted to share this love of my city with all my customers. The décor at Mother India is full of Glasgow's history, its inhabitants and its heritage, and that lends itself to a unique atmosphere. Our local customers particularly find comfort in its friendly familiarity and those who travel from further afield to visit us are struck by the 'Scottishness' they find in an Indian restaurant. I don't think many other restaurants can claim to have such a unique fusion.

Glasgow and Edinburgh are impressively multicultural cities and our customers reflect their diversity. There is no 'typical' Mother India customer and I love that. One of the joys of Indian food and culture is that it breaks down boundaries. There is no pretence, formality or ceremony at mealtimes and our food is more accessible to a wider spectrum of budgets than almost any other type of cuisine. People from all walks of life rub elbows at our tables and they tuck into their meals with the same vigour, enthusiasm and enjoyment. I want the Mother India Cookbook to reflect what it's like to eat at one of Mother India's restaurants, cafes or delis.

the den

SCALLOPS WITH CAULIFLOWER

Serves 4

For the cauliflower

25ml sunflower oil or light olive oil

1 medium onion, finely chopped

4 cloves of garlic, finely chopped or crushed

1 small knob of fresh ginger

2 green chillies, finely chopped

½ tablespoon roasted cumin seeds (see page 270)

½ teaspoon roasted fennel seeds (see page 270)

2 cloves

2 green cardamom pods

2 ripe tomatoes, skins removed and chopped

½ teaspoon sea salt

¼ teaspoon red chilli powder

½ teaspoon ground turmeric

1 medium new potato, parboiled

1 medium cauliflower, broken into florets

1 tablespoon butter

For the scallops

1 tablespoon olive oil

12–16 plump scallops, out of the shell and coral removed

Heat the oil in a medium pan and add the onion. Cook gently for 5 minutes, until translucent and soft, then add the garlic, ginger and green chillies. Keep cooking over a low–medium heat for a further few minutes, then add the cumin seeds, fennel seeds and cloves. Simmer, stirring, for a few minutes, then add the cardamom pods, tomatoes, salt, chilli powder and turmeric. Stir and simmer again for a few minutes, then add the potato and cauliflower along with the butter. Add a little water if necessary to make sure your cauliflower cooks properly. Cover with a lid and cook for a final 15 minutes, or until the potato and cauliflower are cooked through, adding a little water if the sauce starts to stick to the bottom of the pan.

Meanwhile heat the olive oil in a separate pan. When it sizzles, add the scallops one at a time, searing them for 30 seconds on one side and 20 seconds on the other. Pop the scallops into the pan of cauliflower and tomato sauce and serve immediately, with roti or flatbread.

FINE DICED SALAD

Serves 4 as a side salad

1 red pepper
1 tablespoon sunflower oil
   or light olive oil
16 baby tomatoes (or more,
   if you like extra tomato)
4 sun-dried tomatoes
2 medium red salad onions
1 small bunch of radishes
1 tablespoon good extra
   virgin olive oil (for
   dressing)
1 tablespoon maple syrup
1 tablespoon white wine
   vinegar
1 teaspoon Dijon mustard
½ teaspoon salt
¼ teaspoon red chilli
   powder

Preheat the oven to 190°C/gas mark 6.

Cut the pepper into quarters, discarding the core. Rub with the oil and place on a small baking tray. Roast in the oven for 15 minutes or until soft, then remove from the oven and leave to cool.

Cut the tomatoes into quarters. The sun-dried tomatoes, red onions, radishes and roasted peppers should all be sliced as finely as possible and into equal sizes. Put all the vegetables into a large bowl and mix together.

Whisk the rest of the ingredients together to make a dressing. Pour over the salad and toss gently before serving.

My younger son, Amaan, was born in 2002. Smeena and I found out quite early on that Amaan is autistic. Over the years, he's grown into a lovely, loving boy and we cherish him dearly, but, of course, having an autistic child is not without its challenges. One of the many challenges early on with Amaan was getting him to eat properly. Amaan was a huge fan of takeaways; he loved burgers and chips. I admit that when he was younger it was easier to give in to him, just so that we could get him to eat something, rather than him eating nothing.

In the last few years, I've managed to get Amaan to try my food and he is actually getting to like it a lot, especially Murgh Palau and chicken dishes with rice. Amaan now has much healthier meals, which he loves. Smeena and I see a difference in him too, he seems calmer and more grounded when he's had good home-cooked food, full of nourishment. He's even started cooking lunch alongside me at home on Saturdays.

Having an autistic child has made Smeena and I slow down a little bit. We've come to realise that having a loving family where we can nourish our two sons is the most important thing for us. Of course, I've been extremely lucky, particularly over the last decade or so, and now things really feel like they have fallen into place and it's time to reflect and gather together my favourite recipes; some from Mother India, some from the Den or from the Café, many from my home.

Martin and I have tried in this book to create something a bit unusual by looking at the world of restaurants, cities and home in a different way, taking a 'sideways glance' as Martin would say. My trip to the Punjab changed the way I looked at the roots of Indian home cooking. The idea of taking these principles back home to Scotland, giving them my own twist and making them work in Glaswegian and Edinburgh restaurants was, I think, quite a risk in hindsight. I'm just very relieved I found a way to make this a success. It's been a bit of a rocky road at times, but over the last decade in particular things have gone from strength-to-strength – and I'm very grateful for that. I'm especially grateful to the loyal customers who have helped Mother India to grow and flourish. I'd like to thank all the talented people I've worked with, who have helped along the way. I hope you find this book as interesting as Martin, myself and the great team at Preface have, when putting it all together.

I hope you enjoy cooking and eating these recipes as much as I have enjoyed creating them.

CHICKPEAS WITH STUFFED MUSHROOMS

Serves 4

For the mushrooms

20 large button mushrooms

100g fresh breadcrumbs

30g butter

a small handful of chopped
   fresh parsley

½ teaspoon salt

For the chickpeas

180g dried chickpeas,
   soaked in water overnight

2 tablespoons sunflower oil
   or light olive oil

1 medium onion, finely
   chopped

3 cloves of garlic, finely
   chopped

3 green chillies, finely
   chopped

1 teaspoon roasted cumin
   seeds (see page 270)

½ x 400g tin chopped
   tomatoes

1 teaspoon salt

¼ teaspoon ground
   turmeric

½ teaspoon red chilli
   powder

½ teaspoon garam masala

¼ teaspoon cracked black
   pepper

Take the stems out of the mushrooms. Put the stems into a mini food processor and blend a few times, then transfer to a bowl and add the breadcrumbs, butter, parsley and salt. Mix together, then place a small spoonful of the mixture into each mushroom cap where you removed the stem.

Wash the chickpeas and place in a pan. Cover with water and bring to the boil, then reduce the heat and simmer for 30 minutes to an hour, or until the chickpeas are nice and soft. Drain and set aside.

Preheat the oven to 180°C/gas mark 6.

Heat the oil in an ovenproof pan or casserole dish. Once hot, add the onion and cook gently for 10 minutes stirring every now and then. Add the garlic, green chillies and cumin seeds. Cook for 3 minutes, then add the tomatoes, salt, turmeric and chilli powder and let everything simmer away for 5 more minutes.

Add the drained chickpeas and cook for 10 minutes, adding a splash of hot water if required to stop everything drying out. Sprinkle over the garam masala and black pepper and place the stuffed mushrooms on top of the chickpeas. Put the dish into the oven for a final 15 minutes.

KOFTA EGG SALAD

Serves 4

For the koftas

350g minced lamb

1 small onion, quartered

2 cloves of garlic

2 green chillies

10 black peppercorns

6 cloves

1 small cinnamon stick

½ tablespoon roasted
   cumin seeds (see page
   270)

40g breadcrumbs

½ tablespoon tomato purée

¾ level tablespoon salt

½ tablespoon paprika

¼ tablespoon red chilli
   powder

a pinch of grated nutmeg

a few sprigs of fresh
   rosemary, leaves finely
   chopped

1 tablespoon oil, for frying

For the egg salad

1 medium red onion, finely
   chopped

16 baby tomatoes, quartered
   (drain any excess juice)

4 oven-roasted tomatoes,
   quartered

1 bunch of small radishes,
   sliced

2 red peppers, roasted and
   sliced (use the ones from
   a jar if you wish)

a handful of mixed salad
   leaves

To make the koftas, place the lamb in a large mixing bowl. Put the onion, garlic and green chillies into a small food processor and pulse until they are chopped but not so much that they turn into a purée. Transfer to a bowl. Crush the peppercorns, cloves and cinnamon stick in a pestle and mortar to a fine powder consistency, then add the cumin seeds and crush a few times, just enough to break the seeds up slightly. Put all these into the bowl of lamb mince, add the breadcrumbs and all the other kofta ingredients apart from the oil, and mix thoroughly to combine. Cover the bowl and refrigerate for 1 hour.

When you're ready to make the koftas, preheat the oven to 220°C/gas mark 7. Shape the mixture into meatballs about the size of a golf ball. Put the oil into a medium non-stick frying pan over a medium heat. Once the oil is hot, carefully add the meatballs, making sure not to overcrowd the pan. Sear for 2 minutes, then, using tongs, flip each meatball over and cook for a further 2 minutes to sear the other side. Remove them to an ovenproof dish and gently press the meatballs with a paper towel before placing them in the oven for about 10 minutes, or until they are cooked through.

To make the salad, put the onion, both kinds of tomatoes, the radishes, peppers and salad leaves into a large bowl. Have a large platter (or 4 individual plates) ready for serving.

To make the dressing, whisk together the oil and lemon juice, then add the salt, pepper, mustard and sugar and give everything another good whisk. Stir in the parsley. Pour over the salad, tossing gently so that everything is evenly coated with the dressing.

Put the salad on to the platter or plates, add the koftas and the eggs, and finally top with the croutons.

4 soft-boiled eggs,
   quartered
a handful of croutons

For the dressing
2 tablespoons extra virgin
   olive oil
juice of 1 small lemon
½ teaspoon salt
¼ teaspoon crushed black
   pepper
½ teaspoon Dijon mustard
½ teaspoon sugar
a handful of fresh flat-leaf
   parsley, chopped

SPICED CULLEN SKINK

Serves 4

500g smoked haddock
(non-dyed is best) and
Arbroath smokies
(optional) (if using both,
use 250g of each)

2 bay leaves

1 blade of mace

a handful of flat-leaf
parsley, leaves and stalks

500ml milk

30g butter

2 small onions, diced

2 cloves of garlic, crushed

1 green chilli, finely
chopped

1 teaspoon roasted cumin
seeds (see page 270)

½ teaspoon roasted
fenugreek seeds (see page
270)

¾ teaspoon salt

2 medium new potatoes,
diced and parboiled

2 tablespoons double
cream

400ml chicken stock (see
page 235) (you can use
vegetable stock if you
want)

½ teaspoon cracked black
pepper

2 handfuls croutons

1 tablespoon chopped fresh
chives

Put the fish, bay leaves, mace and parsley stalks into a very
large pan. Pour over the milk and bring to a simmer, then
leave the fish to poach in the simmering milk for 8–10 minutes.
Remove the fish carefully with a slotted spoon and set aside to
cool.

Once cool, remove the skin and discard and flake the fish.
Strain the milk through a sieve into a bowl or another pan, and
reserve for later.

Melt the butter in a frying pan over a medium heat and add
the onions. Cook gently for 5–8 minutes, being careful not to
let the onions brown, then add the garlic, chilli, cumin seeds,
fenugreek seeds and salt. Cook for 2 more minutes, then add the
potatoes and mix well. Cook for 5 minutes more, then add the
milk you poached the fish in, plus the cream and chicken stock.
Bring to a simmer, cook for about 5 minutes, then check the
potatoes – they should be soft and cooked through.

Add the flaked fish, parsley leaves and black pepper and
simmer for a minute. Serve immediately, topped with croutons
and chives.

KARELA STUFFED WITH CHANA DAAL

Serves 4

For the chana daal

180g chana daal
½ teaspoon ground
    turmeric
30ml sunflower oil
1 small onion, finely
    chopped
3 cloves of garlic, sliced
1 green chilli, sliced
½ teaspoon cumin seeds
1 teaspoon salt
½ teaspoon red chilli
    powder
½ teaspoon garam masala

For the karela

6–8 karelas (bitter melons)
3 tablespoons sunflower oil
20g butter
1 medium onion, sliced
2 cloves of garlic, sliced
20g fresh ginger, chopped
2 plum tomatoes, deseeded,
    chopped
1 teaspoon salt
¼ teaspoon ground
    turmeric
½ teaspoon red chilli
    powder
a handful of fresh
    coriander leaves

Soak the chana daal in water for 2 hours. Drain and rinse, then put into a pan and add 700ml water. Bring to the boil, skimming off any froth that rises to the surface, then add the turmeric and cook for about 30 minutes, or until the daal is fully cooked. Strain through a fine colander.

Put the oil into a separate pan over a medium heat. Once hot, add the onion and cook gently for 2 minutes, then add the garlic, green chilli and cumin. Cook gently for a further 2 minutes, then add the salt and chilli powder. Cook for 1 minute, adding a splash of water if required, then add the cooked chana daal and mix well. Cook for a final 5 minutes, then add the garam masala. The chana daal should be quite dry at this stage.

Prepare the karelas by peeling away all the rough skin until each gourd is smooth. Slit open the side and remove all the seeds so that each karela is completely empty inside, then carefully stuff with the cooked chana daal. You will need a few small cocktail sticks to secure the karelas once stuffed (see illustration).

Heat half the oil in a large non-stick pan. Once hot, carefully add the karelas with the stuffed side facing upwards, and sear the bottom and sides for about 5 minutes. The skin should turn slightly brown. Depending on the size of your pan (and the karelas) you may need to do this in two batches. Once all the karelas are cooked, lift them carefully out of the pan and place them on a plate covered with a sheet of kitchen paper.

Give the pan a wipe and add the remaining oil and the butter. Once hot, add the onion, garlic and ginger. Cook for 2 minutes and add the tomatoes, salt, turmeric and chilli powder. Cook for a further 2 minutes, then stir in the coriander and mix well. Put the stuffed karelas back into the pan one at a time to heat through.

Serve with wholemeal chapatis and a salad.

LAHORE FISH STEW

Serves 4

20ml sunflower oil

1 small onion, chopped

2 garlic cloves, finely
   chopped

2 pieces of stem ginger

2 green chillies, finely
   chopped

½ teaspoon roasted cumin
   seeds (see page 270)

½ teaspoon roasted fennel
   seeds (see page 270)

1 x 400g tin of tomatoes

1 x 400g tin of chickpeas,
   drained

400ml vegetable stock

1 star anise

1 teaspoon salt

450g mixed king prawns,
   monkfish, cod and sea
   bass cut into 2cm cubes

½ teaspoon cracked black
   pepper

Put the oil into a large pan over a medium heat. Once hot, add the onion and cook gently for a few minutes, until soft, then add the garlic, stem ginger and green chillies. Cook for a further 2 minutes, making sure not to let the onion brown, then add the cumin seeds, fennel seeds, tinned tomatoes and half the chickpeas. Simmer for another 5 minutes, then add half the vegetable stock.

Carefully put this mixture into a heatproof blender and blend until smooth. Put the blended mixture back into the pan and add the remaining chickpeas and stock, with the star anise and salt. Bring back to a simmer. After it has been simmering for 5 minutes, add the seafood, starting with the king prawns and monkfish, and poach gently for about 5 minutes, or until all the seafood is fully cooked and opaque-looking.

Season with black pepper and serve with naan bread.

WHOLE STEAMED CHICKEN STUFFED WITH SMOKED AUBERGINE

Serves 4–6

For the smoked aubergine

1 tablespoon sunflower oil
1 small onion, finely diced
1 clove of garlic, crushed
1 plum tomato, deseeded
  and chopped
¾ teaspoon salt
4 small smoked aubergines
  (see page 279)
½ teaspoon black pepper
30g breadcrumbs

For the chicken

1 chicken, approx. 1.5kg
50ml vegetable oil
2 medium onions, chopped
8 cloves of garlic, chopped
1 knob of fresh ginger,
  chopped
6 green chillies, finely
  chopped
¾ tablespoon roasted
  cumin seeds
6 black peppercorns
4 cloves
1 large cinnamon stick
2 black cardamom pods
1 x 400g tin of chopped
  tomatoes
¾ tablespoon tomato purée
1 tablespoon salt
½ tablespoon ground
  turmeric
¾ tablespoon red chilli
  powder
50g butter

To make the stuffing, first heat the oil in a medium sauté pan. Once hot, add the onion and garlic and cook gently for 2 minutes, then add the tomato and salt and cook for a further 2 minutes. Add the smoked aubergines and cook for another 2 minutes, then season with the black pepper. Remove from the heat and allow to cool, then mix in the breadcrumbs. Score the skin of the chicken with a sharp knife. Push the aubergine stuffing into the cavity until it's full, then tie the legs together with string, and truss the whole chicken.

Put the oil into a pan large enough to fit the chicken and place on the heat. When hot, add the onions and cook gently for 10 minutes, then add the garlic, ginger and green chillies. Cook for a further 10 minutes, then add all the whole spices. After another 10 minutes' cooking, add the tinned tomatoes and tomato purée. Let everything simmer away for about 5 minutes, then add the salt, ground turmeric and chilli powder. After a further 5 minutes the mixture should be looking nice and rich.

Add the butter and cook for a further 10 minutes, then put the whole chicken into the pan. Reduce the heat to very low and place a lid on the pan, letting the steam cook the chicken. This usually takes about 1 hour 10 minutes. Make sure you baste the chicken with the sauce every 20–25 minutes to infuse the flavours into the meat. You may need to add a splash of hot water to stop the sauce sticking or burning – a little extra steam also helps the chicken stay juicy and tender.

Preheat the oven to 180°C/gas mark 7. After about 1 hour 10 minutes, remove the whole chicken and the rich sauce from the pot and place everything in a large roasting tray, adding a splash of water if the chicken looks dry. Lay a piece of tin foil loosely over the whole tray and cook in the oven for 15 minutes, then remove the foil and cook for a final 15 minutes. The chicken should be nice and brown. Check that it is cooked right through – if in doubt, pierce some of the thicker parts of the flesh and if the juices run clear the chicken is fully cooked. Serve with salad, rice and baked vegetables.

SMOKED AUBERGINE AND FENUGREEK MASH PIE

Serves 4
500g puff pastry
1 egg, beaten

For the aubergine
1 tablespoon sunflower oil
20g butter
1 medium onion
4 cloves of garlic
2 green chillies
1 tablespoon cumin seeds
2 tablespoons tinned
  chopped tomatoes
1 teaspoon salt
12 baby aubergines,
  smoked following the
  method on page 278
2 oven-cooked tomatoes,
  quartered (see page 275)
½ teaspoon garam masala
½ teaspoon cracked black
  pepper

For the fenugreek mash
30g butter
1 small onion, finely
  chopped
2 cloves of garlic, crushed
30g fresh fenugreek leaves
250ml milk
¾ tablespoon salt
4 medium potatoes, boiled
  with their skins on, then
  mashed
1 teaspoon freshly ground
  white peppercorns

Heat the oil and butter in a large pan. Once hot, add the onion and cook for 2 minutes, then add the garlic, green chillies and cumin. Let everything simmer away for a further 2 minutes, then add the tinned tomatoes and salt. Cook for 2 minutes more, then add the aubergines and keep cooking for a further 5 minutes over a low heat until they are tender but not too soft. Stir in the tomatoes, garam masala and black pepper. Set aside while you prepare the mash.

Preheat the oven to 200°C/gas mark 7. Melt the butter in a medium pan and add the onion and garlic. Cook for about 5–10 minutes, until they are soft but not browned, then add the fenugreek leaves. Mix well to release the flavours and cook over a low–medium heat for 2 minutes. Add the milk and salt and bring to a simmer for a few minutes, then add the mashed potato and stir, seasoning finally with the white pepper. Roll out the puff pastry until about 1cm thick.

Put the cooked aubergine into a baking dish roughly 23cm x 23cm x 8cm and cover with the mash. Top with the pastry, brush with a little eggwash and place in the oven for about 30 minutes, or until the pastry is golden in colour.

Serve with a salad.

BEETROOT AND EGG SALAD

Serves 4

For the salad

3 uncooked beetroots

sea salt

20 baby tomatoes,
    quartered (drain any
    excess juice)

8 radishes, thinly sliced

1 small red onion, finely
    chopped

1 red pepper, roasted and
    chopped

4 medium soft-boiled eggs,
    cut into wedges

handful of mixed salad
    leaves

For the dressing

1 tablespoon virgin olive
    oil

juice of ½ a lemon

1 teaspoon Dijon mustard

1 teaspoon clear honey

¼ teaspoon salt

¼ teaspoon freshly ground
    black pepper

Preheat the oven to 220°C/gas mark 8. Wash the beetroots thoroughly to remove any dirt, but leave the skins on. Allow to dry, then place on a sheet of tin foil and season with sea salt. Bring the sides of the foil up to create a parcel, and roast the beetroots in the oven for 30 minutes, or until they are tender. Remove the parcel from the oven and allow the beetroots to cool down before cutting them into wedges.

Make the dressing by whisking all the ingredients in a large bowl until you have an emulsion. Add all the salad ingredients, except the eggs, and toss to coat in the dressing. Serve in a salad bowl or on a large platter, topped with the eggs and the salad leaves.

LAYERED VEGETABLE BIRYANI

Serves 4

25ml sunflower oil

1 medium onion, finely
  chopped

4 cloves of garlic, finely
  chopped

20g ginger, finely chopped

2 green chillies, sliced

1 teaspoon roasted cumin
  seeds (see page 270)

2 plum tomatoes, chopped

1 teaspoon salt

½ teaspoon red chilli
  powder

¼ teaspoon ground
  turmeric

2 tablespoons yoghurt

4 medium carrots, chopped
  into 2 cm pieces

1 medium cauliflower,
  separated into florets

100g frozen peas

20 button mushrooms

For the rice

400g basmati rice

3 green cardamom pods

2 sticks cinnamon

4 cloves

a few sprigs of fresh mint

1 teaspoon salt

2 tablespoons sunflower oil

To finish

crispy onions (see page
  274)

25g chilled butter

Soak the rice in lukewarm water for 30 minutes, then drain.

Heat the oil in a large pan. Once hot, add the onion and cook gently for 3 minutes, then add the garlic, ginger, green chillies and cumin seeds and cook for a further 3 minutes. Add the tomatoes, salt, chilli powder and turmeric and let everything simmer for a couple of minutes. Whip the yoghurt in a small dish using a whisk to get rid of any lumps and to make it smooth, then add it to the pan and stir well. After 3 minutes of simmering add the carrots and cauliflower, stirring well, then cover the pan with a lid and let the vegetables simmer over a low to medium heat for 10 minutes, checking them every now and then.

Add the peas and mushrooms, stir well, and simmer for a final 2 minutes. You may need a splash of water to stop the mixture sticking to the bottom of the pan. The vegetables should be about two-thirds cooked and al dente at this stage.

Preheat the oven to 180°C/gas mark 6. Pour 2.5 litres of water into a large pan and add the cardamoms, cinnamon stick, cloves, mint, salt and oil. Bring to the boil, then reduce to a simmer for 20 minutes. Add the rice, bring to a simmer for 3 minutes (we want the rice al dente), then drain.

Put a layer of rice into an ovenproof dish about 23cm x 23cm x 10cm. Add a layer of vegetables, then some crispy onions. Repeat the process, finishing with rice as the final layer. Place the butter on top and cover with a lid or tin foil. Place in the oven and bake for 40 minutes.

Serve with raita and a salad.

LAMB SAGALUM (Lamb Chops with Baby Turnips)

Serves 4

3 tablespoons sunflower oil
  or light olive oil
2 small to medium onions,
  finely diced
6 cloves of garlic, finely
  chopped
50g fresh ginger, finely
  chopped
5 medium green chillies,
  finely chopped
a small handful of fresh
  coriander, chopped
1 level teaspoon cumin
  seeds
10 crushed black
  peppercorns
3 cloves
1 cinnamon stick
2 green cardamom pods
½ x 400g tin of tomatoes
¾ teaspoon of salt (or less
  if you prefer)
1 level teaspoon ground
  turmeric
½ tablespoon of chilli
  powder
8 good-sized lamb chops
4 oven dried tomatoes,
halved (sun-dried if you
prefer)

For the turnips

2 tablespoons sunflower oil
  or light olive oil
3 shallots, or 1 small onion,
  finely diced

Heat the oil in a large heavy-based pan. When it is hot, add the onions and cook over a medium heat for 10 minutes, until translucent and soft but not brown. Add the garlic, ginger, green chillies and coriander and cook gently for a further 10 minutes, stirring occasionally.

In a separate pan over a medium heat, dry-fry the cumin seeds, peppercorns, cloves, cinnamon stick and cardamom pods for a couple of minutes, until the cumin seeds turn slightly darker. Be careful not to burn the spices, as this will impair their flavour.

After the onion mixture has been cooking for 10 minutes, add the toasted whole spices to the pan. Keep stirring when necessary and add a tablespoon of water if anything looks as if it's starting to stick. Stir in the tinned tomatoes and simmer gently for 5 minutes, then add the salt, turmeric and chilli powder. Now your base is ready, so all you've got to do is add the lamb chops to the sauce and mix well, then simmer gently, covered, for a further 30 minutes, turning every 8–10 minutes so that all the chops cook through. Add a splash of water if the chops look dry.

Meanwhile cook the turnips. Heat the oil in a medium-large frying pan. Add the shallots or onion, along with the garlic, and fry gently for about 10 minutes, until soft and translucent. Pop the green chillies into the pan, season with salt, then simmer for 5 minutes, stirring occasionally. Stir in the diced turnips and cook for a further 10 minutes, or until cooked through but still firm. Add the salt and pepper and keep warm.

Preheat the oven to 200°C/gas mark 7.

When the chops are cooked, transfer the contents of your pan to a large baking tray. Carefully place a tomato half on top of each chop, then put back into the oven and cook for a final 7–10 minutes to bring all the flavours together.

Serve the lamb with the turnips.

2 cloves of garlic, finely
  chopped
2 green chillies, finely
  chopped
4 small turnips, peeled and
  diced to about 1cm
½ teaspoon salt
½ teaspoon freshly cracked
  black pepper

This dish works really well with plain basmati rice and/or Indian flatbreads like chapati and naan. Mild cucumber raita is also a great accompaniment – the cooling freshness and creamy texture of this traditional Indian staple with the gently spiced meatiness of the lamb is a match made in heaven.

FISH AND POTATO PAKORAS

Serves 4

1 medium onion, finely
  diced
2 medium potatoes,
  parboiled and medium
  diced
2 green chillies, finely
  chopped
½ tablespoon roasted
  cumin seeds (see page
  270)
½ tablespoon crushed
  coriander seeds
½ tablespoon dried
  fenugreek leaves
¼ tablespoon chilli powder
¼ tablespoon ground
  turmeric
½ tablespoon salt
225g gram flour
2 skinless haddock fillets,
  cut into bite-size pieces
vegetable oil, for deep-
  frying

Put the onion, potatoes and green chillies into a large bowl with all the spices and salt, mix well, then set aside for 30 minutes. Add the gram flour and then add water a little at a time until you have a batter. The consistency should be such that the vegetables are just clinging together and no more – so not too thick and not too thin. Now gently fold in the pieces of haddock, trying not to break up the fish.

Heat the vegetable oil to 160°C in a deep-fryer, or pour the oil into a very large pan, to come one third of the way up the sides, and heat to 160°C. Keep an oven glove nearby, and a lid in case the oil gets too hot and starts to spit. We recommend using the fryer option, if you have one, as you can control the temperature and the whole process is much safer.

Lift out a good tablespoon of batter, making sure you include a couple of chunks of haddock, and use a second tablespoon to slowly slide the batter off into the oil. Do this as close to the oil as is safely possible. It is actually more dangerous to plop it in from too far away, as you will increase the risk of splashing. Fry for about 2–3 minutes, until crisp and golden. Cook about 6 pakoras at a time so that they cook evenly and you don't crowd your pan.

Using a dry slotted spoon, remove the pakoras from the oil and place them on a plate lined with kitchen paper to absorb any excess oil. Eat while warm, and serve with raita and salad.

CINNAMON AND BLACK PEPPER CHICKEN

Serves 4

50ml sunflower oil
1 medium onion, finely
  chopped
3 cinnamon sticks
25 black peppercorns
4 black cardamom pods
12 cloves
3 green chillies, finely
  chopped
½ tablespoon cumin seeds
1 tablespoon garlic purée
  (see page 273)
¾ x 400g tin of chopped
  tomatoes
1 tablespoon tomato purée
1 tablespoon salt
1 whole medium/large
  chicken, cut into 8 pieces
  (skin removed, but keep
  the bones in)
20g butter

Heat the oil in a medium ovenproof pan and add the onion. Cook gently for 1 minute, then add the cinnamon sticks, peppercorns, cardamoms, cloves and green chillies. Cook for 5 minutes, until the onions are golden, then add the cumin seeds. Cook, stirring, for a further 2 minutes, then add 100ml of hot water. Add the garlic purée and cook for 5 minutes, then add the tinned tomatoes, tomato purée and the salt.

Cook for 5 more minutes, stirring occasionally, until the sauce thickens, then add the chicken pieces. Stir well, cover the pan with a lid, and turn the heat down low. Cook for 15 minutes, then add the butter and stir again and replace the lid.

Meanwhile, preheat the oven to 200°C/gas mark 7. Cook the chicken and sauce on the hob for a further 10 minutes with the lid on, then remove the lid, put the pan into the oven and cook for 15 minutes, or until the chicken is cooked through and the juices run clear. (If the chicken pieces are large you may need to let it cook for a little longer.)

Serve with boiled baby potatoes and salad. It's also delicious with homemade chips if you're feeling a bit more decadent.

LAMB RAAN

Ask your butcher to trim the end of the bone (the knuckle bit), and also to cut the lamb joint just above the shank so that the whole leg will fit into a large pan.

Serves 4–6

25ml sunflower oil

2 medium onions, finely chopped

10 cloves of garlic, finely chopped

6 green chillies, finely chopped

1 large knob of fresh ginger, chopped

15 black peppercorns

8 cloves

2 cinnamon sticks

2 pieces of mace

¾ tablespoon roasted cumin seeds (see page 270)

¾ x 400g tin of tomatoes

1 tablespoon tomato purée

1½ tablespoons salt

1 tablespoon red chilli powder

½ tablespoon ground turmeric

20g butter

100ml water

1 whole leg of lamb, approx. 2kg, on the bone

½ tablespoon brown sugar (optional)

25g whole almonds (optional)

Heat the oil in a pan large enough for the leg of lamb to fit into, and add the onions. Cook gently for 5 minutes, until translucent and soft, then add the garlic, green chillies and ginger. Keep cooking over a low–medium heat for a further 5 minutes, then add the peppercorns, cloves, cinnamon sticks, mace and cumin seeds. Stir thoroughly and cook for another 5 minutes, then add the tinned tomatoes and tomato purée. Cook for a further 5 minutes and then season with the salt, chilli powder and turmeric.

After another 2 minutes add the butter and 100ml water, and finally the leg of lamb. Turn the heat down to low, then cover with a lid and let the lamb slowly cook for 90 minutes, turning it over every 30 minutes. Add some hot water every now and then to create steam so that the lamb doesn't dry out.

Preheat the oven to 190°C/gas mark 6. After 90 minutes, transfer the lamb and onions to a large roasting tray and cover with foil. Roast for 20 minutes, then carefully remove the lamb from the oven and sprinkle the brown sugar and almonds over the top if using. Put the lamb back into the oven without any foil for 10 minutes, or until the sugar has caramelised.

Serve with roast potatoes and vegetable apple chutney.

SINDHI CHICKEN PIE

Serves 4
1 x 500g packet of puff
    pastry
1 egg, for glazing

For the mashed potato
4 potatoes (such as
    Desiree), peeled and
    cut into equal-sized
    pieces
½ tablespoon salt
50g butter
2 cloves of garlic, finely
    chopped
150ml whole milk
2 cardamom pods, crushed
2 teaspoons salt
½ teaspoon cracked black
    pepper

For the chicken
50ml sunflower oil
1 medium onion, finely
    chopped
4 cloves of garlic, crushed
4 green chillies, finely
    chopped
½ tablespoon salt
½ tablespoon roasted
    cumin seeds
½ tablespoon roasted
    fenugreek seeds
2 ripe tomatoes, chopped
1 teaspoon ground turmeric
4 small chicken breast
    fillets (about 800g in
    total), cut into 1cm pieces
a handful of flat-leaf parsley

Put the potatoes into a medium saucepan and cover them with cold water. Add ½ tablespoon salt and bring to a simmer, then put a lid on the pan and cook for around 15 minutes, or until the potatoes are soft. Once cooked, drain the potatoes and allow them to dry in the pan while you prepare the chicken.

Heat the sunflower oil in a large sauté pan. When the oil is hot, add the onion and cook for 3 minutes, then add the garlic, green chillies, salt, cumin seeds and fenugreek seeds. Cook for 5 minutes, then add the tomatoes and turmeric. Cook for a further 2 minutes, then add the chicken. Mix well and cook for about 5 minutes, or until the chicken is completely cooked through. Once the chicken is done, stir in the parsley.

Now make the mash. Melt the butter in a medium pan over a low heat. Add the garlic and sauté for about 1–2 minutes, then add the milk and the cardamom pods and simmer gently for about 3–4 minutes. Add the potatoes, salt and pepper and mash to as smooth a consistency as possible. Allow the mash and chicken mixture to cool slightly, as the puff pastry will just melt if you place it on top of hot pie mixture.

Preheat the oven to 180°C/gas mark 6. Once the mash and chicken mixture have cooled down a bit, layer them in a loaf tin or ovenproof dish, the chicken first, with the mash on top. Roll out the puff pastry to a thickness of about 5mm. Place it over the pie and make a small hole in the middle, then make criss-cross slashes in the pastry and finally brush it with the eggwash. Bake in the middle of the oven for about 30 minutes, or until the pastry is cooked through and golden in colour.

Serve with a salad.

OMELETTE WITH SMOKED HADDOCK AND SALMON

Serves 2

1 tablespoon sunflower oil
100g salmon fillet, skin off
100g smoked haddock
  fillet, skin off
20g butter
1 shallot, finely chopped
½ teaspoon cumin seeds
4 spring onions, finely
  chopped
1 heaped tablespoon green
  peas
1 green chilli, finely
  chopped
a few sprigs of fresh
  coriander, leaves finely
  chopped
4 eggs, lightly beaten with
  ¾ teaspoon salt

Start by cooking the fish. Put the oil into a non-stick pan over a medium–high heat. When the oil is hot, add the salmon and sear on both sides. Add the smoked haddock to the salmon a minute later. Cook for a further 2 minutes, then turn over for a further minute, or until the fish is just cooked and no more.

Remove the fish from the pan and set aside. Add the butter and shallot to the pan (if it is very greasy from the salmon, simply wipe any excess oil away before adding the butter). Cook the shallot over a gentle heat for a minute, then add the cumin. Keep the heat medium–low so that the shallot doesn't brown. Add the spring onions, peas, green chilli and coriander, mix everything well with a wooden spoon and pan-fry for another 2 minutes.

Preheat the grill to a high setting so it's ready for finishing the omelette.

Now add the beaten eggs to the pan, keeping the heat low while gently stirring. After 20 seconds place the salmon and haddock on top and pop the pan under the grill for about 1 minute, or until the omelette is soft and fluffy.

Serve immediately while warm, with toast.

SPINACH WITH ROASTED BUFFALO PANEER

Serves 2

10g butter

2 tablespoons sunflower oil

1 medium onion, finely chopped

3 cloves of garlic, finely chopped

a small knob of fresh ginger, finely chopped

1 green chilli, finely chopped

12g fresh fenugreek leaves

½ teaspoon roasted cumin seeds (see page 270)

2 cloves

1 small cinnamon stick

¼ x 400g tin of tomatoes

½ tablespoon salt

¼ teaspoon ground turmeric

¼ tablespoon red chilli powder

200g frozen spinach, defrosted

a handful of fresh spinach leaves

a handful of fresh coriander

a pinch of freshly grated nutmeg

175g paneer (see page 66)

Heat the butter and 1 tablespoon of sunflower oil in a medium ovenproof pan and add the onion. Cook gently for 5–10 minutes, until translucent and soft, then add the garlic, ginger, green chilli and fenugreek. Keep cooking over a low–medium heat for a further 5 minutes, then add the cumin seeds, cloves and cinnamon stick. Simmer for 2 more minutes, then add the tinned tomatoes and cook for a further 5 minutes. Add the salt, turmeric and red chilli powder and simmer for a few more minutes, then add the defrosted spinach.

Cover with a lid and cook for 25 minutes, stirring occasionally, adding water if needed to loosen the mixture. Finally add the fresh spinach leaves, along with the coriander and nutmeg.

Preheat the oven to 190°C/gas mark 6. Heat the remaining tablespoon of oil in a non-stick pan, and when it is hot add the paneer. Cook for 1 minute, then flip it over and cook for another minute. Place the hot paneer on top of the spinach, then put the pan into the oven, without its lid, and cook for 5 minutes.

Serve with bread and rice.

SHISH KEBAB

Serves 4

1kg finely minced lamb
1 medium onion
1 medium potato
2 slices of bread
1 tablespoon dry fenugreek
    leaves
1 teaspoon roasted cumin
    seeds (see page 270)
1 teaspoon garam masala
½ tablespoon red chilli
    powder
¼ teaspoon freshly grated
    nutmeg
¾ tablespoon salt
4 green chillies, finely
    chopped
a handful of fresh
    coriander, chopped

Preheat the oven to 200°C/gas mark 7 or heat a barbecue until the embers turn grey.

Place the minced lamb in a large bowl. Grate the onion and potato in a food processor and put into a separate bowl, squeezing out any excess liquid. Whiz the 2 slices of bread to breadcrumbs and add to the onion and potato mixture. Put into the large bowl with the minced lamb and add all the spices, salt, green chillies and coriander. Mix well to evenly distribute all the ingredients.

Take handfuls of the kebab mixture and wrap them around wooden skewers, about 16cm long. Either barbecue the kebabs until they are golden brown and are cooked all the way through, or place the skewers on an oiled baking sheet and roast in the oven for 15 minutes.

Serve with raita and basmati rice or naan bread, plus a finely chopped salad.

PAPRIKA LAMB GIGOTS

You need to start preparing this recipe the night before you plan to serve it.

For the marinade

3 tablespoons malt vinegar

2 tablespoons mustard oil
or olive oil

1 tablespoon paprika

¾ tablespoon salt

½ tablespoon red chilli
powder

½ tablespoon roasted
cumin seeds (see page
270)

24 black peppercorns,
crushed

12 cloves, crushed

a pinch of freshly grated
nutmeg

For the lamb

4 lamb gigot chops
(approx. 225g each)

2 tablespoons olive oil

20–25 baby mushrooms

8 shallots, quartered

1 teaspoon smoked paprika

20g butter

200ml hot chicken stock
(see page 235)

Put all the marinade ingredients into a medium bowl and whisk together until the mixture resembles a paste. Add the lamb gigot chops and make sure they are fully coated in the marinade. Cover with clingfilm and leave in the fridge overnight.

The next day, preheat the oven to 200°C/gas mark 7.

Place a large non-stick pan over a medium–high heat and add the olive oil. Once the oil is hot, add the lamb chops. If you can't get them all into the pan, do them in batches. Don't worry about draining off the marinade, as it's quite a dry one and should mostly have soaked into the meat. Sear each gigot on one side for about 4 minutes over a medium heat. Then turn over and sear the other side for about 3 minutes.

Place the gigots in a roasting tin or tray, reserving the non-stick pan for later, and cover loosely with tin foil. Cook in the oven for 20 minutes, then remove and return the lamb to the original non-stick pan. Add the mushrooms and shallots, sprinkle over the smoked paprika and add the butter. Let everything simmer for 5 minutes, or until the shallots have begun to caramelise and the mushrooms are beginning to brown. Pour in the hot chicken stock and simmer for a further 2 minutes.

Serve with potatoes and/or salad.

WEDDING DAY STEAMED CHICKEN WITH VEGETABLES

Serves 4

sunflower oil, for deep-
  frying
4 chicken legs, drumsticks
  and thighs attached, skin
  scored
¼ tablespoon roasted
  cumin seeds (see page
  270)
½ tablespoon black
  peppercorns
6 cloves
4 green cardamom pods
2 tablespoons plain yoghurt
juice of ½ a lemon
6 cloves garlic, crushed
¼ tablespoon fresh green
  chilli, chopped
½ tablespoon salt
¼ tablespoon red chilli
  powder
a mixture of seasonal
  vegetables (cabbage and
  turnips are great, but use
  whatever you like)
a few whole spices, such as
  cumin and coriander
  seeds

Heat the sunflower oil to 150°C in a deep fat fryer or a large pan filled one-third of the way up. Add the chicken legs and deep-fry until they are fully cooked – this should take about 15 minutes. Remove from the oil and check that the juices run clear when you stick a fork deep into the joints. Once cooked, set the chicken aside to cool.

Put the cumin seeds, black peppercorns, cloves and cardamoms into a pestle and mortar and roughly crush. Discard the green shells of the cardamom pods.

Put the yoghurt and lemon juice into a medium bowl and add the garlic, green chilli, salt and chilli powder. Stir in the freshly ground spices and whisk everything together until evenly mixed. Add the cooled chicken and leave to marinate for an hour.

Cut the vegetables into equal sized pieces so they will all cook in the same length of time.

Pour 500ml of water into a steamer, add a few whole spices such as cumin and coriander seeds, and bring to a simmer. Place the chicken and vegetables on the top tray of the steamer, cover with the lid, and steam for about 35 minutes.

Serve with a salad.

HERB-CRUSTED SALMON

Serves 4

4 salmon fillets

½ lemon, cut into wedges

For the marinade

1 tablespoon light olive oil

2 cloves of garlic, finely
  chopped

½ teaspoon each of salt
  and black pepper

For the herb crust

2 slices of stale bread

1 small, fresh coconut,
  grated (or 170–225g
  dessicated coconut)

30g butter

a handful of chopped,
  fresh parsley

1 teaspoon garam masala

½ teaspoon salt

Put the oil, garlic, salt and pepper into a bowl. Add the salmon fillets and turn to coat in the marinade. Cover the bowl with clingfilm and pop it into the fridge for 1 hour.

Preheat the oven to 190°C /gas mark 6.

To make the herb crust, whiz the bread to breadcrumbs in a food processor, put into a bowl, and mix in the rest of the herb crust ingredients.

Remove the bowl of salmon fillets from the fridge and take them out of the marinade. Put them on a baking tray and place even amounts of the herb crust on top of each fillet. Roast in the oven for about 20 minutes, or until the salmon is cooked through.

Serve with a green salad or lemon and cashew nut rice and a wedge of lemon.

MONKFISH KEBABS

Serves 4

2 tablespoons mustard oil
   or olive oil
Juice of a small lemon
½ tablespoon tikka paste
3 green chillies (crushed)
¾ tablespoon salt
½ teaspoon red chilli
   powder
12 black peppercorns
6 cloves
¾ tablespoon cumin seeds,
   roasted
½ tablespoon fennel seeds,
   roasted
600g to 650g monkfish cut
   into 4 cm cubes
1 red pepper, cut into 4 cm
   cubes
1 green pepper, cut into 4
   cm cubes
1 onion, cut into 4 cm cubes
1 ½ tablespoons olive oil
16 whole mushrooms

In a large bowl, mix the oil, lemon juice, tikka paste, green chillies, salt and the red chilli powder. In the mortar, put the peppercorns and cloves and start to crush with the pestle. After a minute add the cumin seeds and fennel seeds and give a few turns with the pestle, just to slightly bruise them, then add to the bowl and mix everything together. Add the monkfish, peppers and the onion and make sure everything is covered with spice mixture. Cover the bowl and place in the fridge for an hour.

Thread the fish, pepper and onion as evenly as you can along 4 wooden skewers.

Preheat your oven to 200C/gas mark 6.

Heat a large pan then add 1 ½ tablespoons of olive oil. Once hot add the skewers and the whole mushrooms. Cook one side for one minute then flip over cook the other side for a minute (you may have to do this in 2 batches), then place in the oven for about 5 minutes or until the fish is cooked.

Serve with saffron mash and salad.

CAULIFLOWER POTATO AND PANEER TART

For the tart
10-inch tart tin
350g shortcrust pastry
   (shop bought is fine)

For the filling
3 tablespoons sunflower oil
medium onion, chopped
1 ½ teaspoons garlic purée
1 knob ginger, chopped
3 green chillies finely
   diced
1 teaspoon salt
½ teaspoon turmeric
½ teaspoon garam masala
½ teaspoon nutmeg
2 plum tomatoes (skinned
   and deseeded)
3 medium potatoes diced
   into 2 cm cubes
small cauliflower cut into
   small florets
½ teaspoon cracked black
   pepper
150g paneer (sliced)

Preheat your oven to 200C/gas mark 6.

Start by blind baking the pastry. Roll out the pastry carefully to about the thickness of a pound coin, then lift up and place over the tart tin and carefully press down. If any cracks or gaps appear in the pastry, press together until the base and sides are covered. Lightly prick the pastry with a fork, then cover with a kitchen towel and place in the freezer for 30 minutes. Remove from the freezer, cover the pastry with parchment paper and place baking beans or chick peas on top, and bake for 15 minutes. Once it is baked, remove the baking beans or chickpeas, but keep them for blind baking in future.

For the filling, add the oil to a large warmed pan. Add the onion, cook for about 8 minutes then add the garlic, ginger, and the green chillies and cook for a further 3 minutes. Then add the salt, turmeric, garam masala, nutmeg and tomatoes and cook for a further 3 minutes. Add the potato and cauliflower, then mix everything together before adding the black pepper. Cover with a lid and cook on a low heat for about 15 minutes, then take the lid off (we want the mixture to be quite dry). You might need to increase the heat to dry it out slightly.

Remove the pan from the heat once you have quite a dry mixture. To get rid of any excess oil in the filling, tip the pan at an angle (see getting started) so any excess oil comes to one side and remove it using a spoon.

Preheat the oven to 200C/ gas mark 6.

Once the filling is cool put it into the tart and place in the oven. Bake for 15 minutes then remove from oven and place the paneer on top. Put back in the oven for a further 15 minutes to roast the paneer. Serve with a nice green salad.

PEA AND ROASTED PANEER SOUP

Serves 4

For the paneer marinade

2 tablespoons double
    cream
1 tablespoon yoghurt
½ teaspoon salt
1 teaspoon white
    peppercorns, crushed
1 x 200g pack paneer, cut
    into quarters
1 teaspoon sugar

For the soup

3 tablespoons sunflower oil
1 small onion, finely
    chopped
4 cloves of garlic, finely
    chopped
2 green chillies, finely
    chopped
1 teaspoon roasted cumin
    seeds (see page 270)
2 green cardamom pods
½ tablespoon salt
1 small potato, diced
200g frozen peas
850ml hot vegetable stock
    or chicken stock (see
    page 235)
¼ teaspoon black
    peppercorns, crushed

Preheat the oven to 200°C/gas mark 7.

Put the cream, yoghurt, salt and white peppercorns into a small bowl and whisk together. Add the paneer and stir so that it is all coated. Drain off any excess coating and place the pieces of paneer on a baking tray. Sprinkle with the sugar and roast in the oven for 15 minutes.

Meanwhile, heat the oil in a medium pan. Once hot, add the onion. Cook gently for 2 minutes, then add the garlic, green chillies, cumin seeds, cardamoms, salt and potato. After 5 minutes add most of the peas and the hot stock. Let everything simmer away for 5 minutes. Cool a little, then put the mixture into a food processor and blend until nice and smooth, being careful to avoid any hot splashes.

Return the blended mixture to the pan, add the rest of the peas, and warm through again but do not bring to the boil. Season with the black pepper and serve in bowls, with the roasted paneer on top.

MAKI ROTI (Corn Flatbread)

Maki roti is a delicious flatbread and is traditionally served with a spinach (saag) side.

Makes 8 flatbreads

300g fine cornmeal (from
    Asian stores)
1 teaspoon ajwain seeds
    (lovage seeds)
½ teaspoon salt
350ml warm water
ghee, for frying

You will need a tava (see
page 268) or a non-stick
frying pan to make these.

Put the cornmeal, ajwain and salt into a bowl and mix together.
Add half the warm water and knead well, adding more water as
required, making sure the dough is smooth and firm but not too
soft. Form into 8 balls.

Heat up a tava or non-stick frying pan while you prepare the
roti. Place a sheet of greaseproof paper on a worktop. Sprinkle
a little water on the paper, then put a ball of dough in the centre
and sprinkle a little more water on top. Cover with another
sheet of greaseproof paper, then press down with a flat (roughly
23–25cm) plate until the bread is about the same thickness as a
pound coin.

Add ½ teaspoon of ghee to the hot tava, then add the flatbread,
lifting it very carefully. Don't worry if it breaks or if cracks
appear, just gently pat it together and it should hold. Once the
bottom is slightly brown, flip over the bread with a spatula (not
by hand). When the other side is browning, flip it again. Cook
until the bread is yellowy golden brown on both sides. Make the
rest of the roti the same way. Remember to pour some ghee on
the sides of the roti while you're cooking it. Wrap the cooked roti
in a tea towel to keep them warm.

Serve hot with spinach, and melt some butter on top of the
spinach if you're feeling decadent.

MILLET CHAPATIS (gluten-free)

This is a healthy version of a chapati made with millet (bajari) flour. In India it's sometimes referred to as farmers' bread.

Makes 8 chapatis
300g millet flour
200g plain yoghurt
2 tablespoons vegetable oil
300ml water

You will need a tava (see page 268) or a flat, heavy-based pan to make these.

Put the millet flour, yoghurt and oil into a medium bowl and mix together. Add the water slowly, just enough to make a dough that's smooth but not too soft. Once the dough is ready, cover with clingfilm or a tea towel and set aside for 15 minutes.

Uncover the dough and divide it into 8 equal-sized balls. Heat the tava on a medium heat for about 10 minutes while you prepare the chapatis. Place a sheet of greaseproof paper on a worktop. Sprinkle a little water on the paper, then put a ball of dough in the centre and sprinkle a little more water on top. Cover with another sheet of greaseproof paper, then press down with a flat (roughly 23–25cm) plate until you have made a flat, round chapati.

Place the chapati on the hot tava until it is completely cooked through and there are no traces of any raw dough. Turn several times during cooking. Make the rest of the chapatis the same way.

Serve with butter.

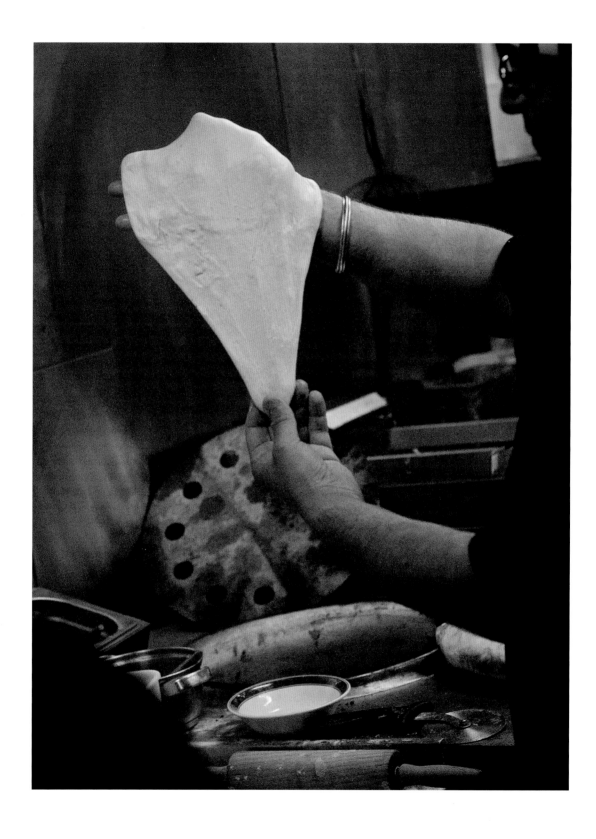

CHICKEN KOFTAS WITH RICE AND POTATO STEW

Serves 4
For the koftas
1 small onion
2 green chillies
400g minced chicken
20g breadcrumbs
1 teaspoon roasted cumin
  seeds (see page 270)
1 teaspoon garam masala
½ tablespoon salt
¼ tablespoon red chilli
  powder
a pinch of freshly grated
  nutmeg
a handful of fresh flat-leaf
  parsley
1 tablespoon sunflower oil

For the stew
2 tablespoons light olive oil
1 small onion, finely
  chopped
2 cloves of garlic, finely
  chopped
20g fresh ginger, chopped
½ x 400g tin of chopped
  tomatoes
2 medium waxy potatoes,
  peeled and cut into 2cm
  cubes
1 teaspoon salt
800ml hot chicken stock
  (see page 235)
30g basmati rice
¾ teaspoon crushed black
  peppercorns

To make the koftas, put the onion and green chillies into a mini food processor and pulse together until finely diced. Put into a mixing bowl with all the remaining kofta ingredients (apart from the oil), combine thoroughly, then cover and refrigerate.

To make the stew, pour the olive oil into a medium pan and place on a medium heat. Once the oil is hot, add the onion, garlic and ginger and cook over a medium heat for 5 minutes, then add the tinned tomatoes. After 3 minutes add the potatoes and salt. Cover and cook over a low to medium heat for about 5 minutes, then remove from the hob.

Preheat the oven to 200°C/gas mark 7.

Take the kofta mixture out of the fridge and shape it into meatballs. Put a non-stick pan on the hob and add 1 tablespoon of oil, carefully adding the meatballs one at a time once the oil is hot. Sear the meatballs on each side for about 1 minute, then place them all on a baking tray and bake in the oven for 10 minutes, or until cooked through.

Return the potato stew to the heat and add the koftas, chicken stock and basmati rice. Bring everything back to a simmer, and after 5 minutes check that the potatoes are soft and the rice is cooked through. Season with the black pepper and serve while hot.

CHICKEN STOCK

Makes 2 litres

4.5 litres water
1 small chicken, approx.
 1kg, cut into small pieces,
 skin on
4 shallots
2 whole bulbs of garlic,
 halved horizontally
1 tablespoon salt
25 black peppercorns

Pour 2 litres of water into a large pan or stockpot and bring to the boil. Once boiling, carefully add the chicken. Boil vigorously for 2 minutes, then drain the water from the pan. Place the chicken to one side on a plate or in a bowl and thoroughly wash the pan you blanched it in. Then put the chicken back, plus the rest of the stock ingredients, and pour in the other 2.5 litres of water. Bring slowly to a simmer, then cover partially with a lid so some of the steam can escape and allow to simmer over a gentle heat for 3 hours, topping up with more water if necessary.

Take off the heat and, once cool, leave everything in the pot and place in the fridge for 8 hours or overnight. The next day, slowly bring everything back to a simmer for another 30 minutes.

Cool the stock completely and keep it in the fridge for 4 days, or freeze and use within 2 months.

POTATO PARATHAS

Makes 4–5 parathas

350g fine chapati flour (or plain flour)

275ml water

2 tablespoons sunflower or vegetable oil

3 medium potatoes, boiled in salted water with their skins on

½ tablespoon salt

¼ tablespoon red chilli powder

1 tablespoon dried fenugreek leaves

½ tablespoon ajwain (nice, but not essential, so don't panic if difficult to track down)

¼ tablespoon garam masala

80g butter, melted

You will need a tava (see page 268) or a heavy-based frying pan to make these

Put the flour into a medium bowl. Slowly add the water while kneading with your hands to make a dough. Leave it to rest for 10 minutes, then knead again. Divide the dough into 8–10 equal portions of about 100g each, and place them on a floured baking tray. Coat each one with oil, then cover with clingfilm and put into the fridge.

Peel the potatoes and put them into a bowl. Add the salt and all the spices and mash until the potatoes have absorbed the flavours.

Place a tava or heavy-based pan on a medium heat. Flour your work surface and take the dough out of the fridge. Place one of the balls of dough on the floured surface and press it with your hand until it's about 12cm in diameter. Place a tablespoonful of the spiced potato mash in the middle. Press out a second ball of dough to the same size, then lay it on top of the mash and press the sides to seal (a bit like making fresh ravioli). Now carefully roll the paratha out to double in size. Lift it, shake off the dry flour, then place on the tava or pan. Cook for around 30 seconds on one side, then flip it over and cook the other side. Brush evenly with the butter, then flip the paratha over again and butter the other side. Cook until golden and crispy, and keep them warm whilst you cook the remaining parathas.

Repeat the process until all the parathas are cooked, and serve with raita (see page 277) and green chilli pickle (see page 278).

BEETROOT CHUTNEY

Makes about 1.1kg

450g beetroots, peeled and
chopped
375g cooking apples,
peeled and chopped
400g granulated sugar
400ml white wine vinegar
5 cloves of garlic, crushed
2 teaspoons grated fresh
ginger
2 teaspoons ground cumin
½ teaspoon ground
cinnamon
½ teaspoon ground cloves

Put the beetroots into a pan with 400ml of water. Cover the pan with a lid then bring to the boil and simmer for around 15 minutes. Cook until tender, then drain and leave to one side.

Put the apples into a pan with the sugar, vinegar, garlic, ginger and all the spices, and bring to the boil. Add the cooked beetroots and bring back to the boil, then simmer gently for 1 hour, or until the chutney is nice and thick. Mash with a potato masher to a smooth consistency, or keep as it is if you prefer a chutney with more texture.

Sterilise a large glass jar or several smaller ones and fill with the chutney. Seal, and keep in the fridge once opened. Store in a cool dark place, unopened. The chutney has a storage life of approximately 3 months.

TURKA SAAG (Farmers' Spinach)

Serves 4

1.5kg saag/dried spinach (palak available from Asian/ continental stores)

500g fresh fenugreek leaves

300g fresh mustard leaves

1½ teaspoons salt

8 green chillies, finely chopped

75g cornflour

150g butter

1 teaspoon mustard seeds

5 cloves of garlic, finely chopped

1 small knob of ginger, finely chopped

6 spring onions, chopped

100ml boiling water

a handful of fresh coriander, chopped

Cut the palak, fenugreek and mustard leaves and wash them thoroughly – there is sometimes a lot of dirt on the leaves. Remove the roots and discard. Put all the leaves into a pan, then add 100ml of water, plus the salt and green chillies, and bring to the boil. Once boiling, turn the heat down and cook the mixture thoroughly until it is very dry, being careful not to burn the leaves. When dry, remove from the heat and add the cornflour. Mix well, then mash with a potato masher until the mixture is very fine. Leave to one side.

Heat the butter in a frying pan, add the mustard seeds, garlic and ginger and cook until slightly brown, then add a large handful of spring onions and cook gently over a low heat for 1 hour. Now add the dried-out saag (spinach) to the mixture and cook for a few minutes more. If it seems very dry, add the boiling water and stir until moist again then cover with a lid. Remove from the heat and sprinkle with the chopped coriander and remaining spring onions.

This is traditionally served with maki roti or gluten-free chapatis.

CRUSHED POTATOES WITH MINT CHUTNEY

Serves 4

For the potatoes

550g new potatoes, such as
    Jersey Royals
25g butter
1 medium onion, finely
    chopped
4 cloves of garlic, finely
    chopped
2 green chillies, finely
    chopped
1 teaspoon roasted cumin
    seeds (see page 270)
1 teaspoon salt
¼ teaspoon ground
    turmeric
2 ripe plum tomatoes,
    chopped
½ teaspoon garam masala
6 spring onions, finely
    sliced
lemon pickle

For the mint chutney

20g fresh mint leaves
10g fresh coriander
2 oven-cooked tomatoes
    (see page 275)
1 green chilli
salt and black pepper

Parboil the potatoes in a pan of boiling salted water until they are al dente. Allow them to cool down, then peel and quarter them.

Next make the chutney: blend all the chutney ingredients together in a mini food processor or with a pestle and mortar until you have a rough mixture.

Put the butter into a frying pan over a medium-high heat. Once it has melted, add the onion and garlic and cook gently for 5 minutes, or until the mixture is soft. Add the green chillies, cumin seeds, salt, turmeric and tomatoes. Cook for 5 minutes, then add the parboiled potatoes along with the mint chutney, stirring everything together until the flavours of the chutney have infused the potatoes. Cover with a lid and leave on a very low heat for 2–3 minutes, or until the potatoes are fully cooked.

Lift the lid and add the garam masala and spring onions. Give the mixture a stir, and serve with naan bread and lemon pickle.

LEMON AND CASHEW NUT RICE

Serves 4–6

40ml sunflower oil

1 small onion, sliced

10 black peppercorns

6 cloves

3 green cardamom pods

2 cinnamon sticks

2 green chillies, sliced

½ tablespoon cumin seeds

4 cloves of garlic, crushed

2 sticks of lemongrass

1 tablespoon salt

950ml hot chicken stock
  (see page 235) or water

350g basmati rice

80g cashew nuts, dry
  roasted

Put a wide pan over a medium heat and add the oil. Once hot, add the onion and cook for 1 minute, then add the peppercorns, cloves, cardamoms, cinnamon sticks, green chillies and cumin and let everything caramelise over a low heat. Once the onions are golden brown, pour in 100ml of water and add the garlic, lemongrass and salt. Let everything simmer away for about 3 minutes, then add the chicken stock. Bring to the boil, then reduce the heat to a simmer. Add the rice and stir gently so that it absorbs the liquid. Reduce the heat as the liquid is absorbed.

Preheat the oven to 150°C/gas mark 2. Once all the liquid has been absorbed by the rice, add the cashews, cover the pan with foil and place in the oven for 15 minutes, or until the rice is fully cooked.

Serve as a side dish.

PAKISTANI CARROTS AND PEAS
Pakistani carrots are in season from November to January.

Serves 4

30ml sunflower or light
  olive oil
20g butter
1 medium onion, finely
  chopped
4 cloves of garlic, finely
  chopped
20g fresh ginger, finely
  chopped
2 green chillies, finely
  chopped
6 curry leaves
1 teaspoon roasted cumin
  seeds (see page 270)
1 small cinnamon stick
1 black cardamom pod
3 medium tomatoes,
  chopped
1 teaspoon salt
½ teaspoon ground
  turmeric
½ teaspoon red chilli
  powder
400g Pakistani carrots, cut
  into small pieces
250g frozen peas, defrosted
10 black peppercorns,
  crushed
4 cloves, crushed in a pestle
  and mortar
fresh coriander leaves, to
  serve

Put the sunflower oil into a pan over a medium heat. Once the oil is hot, add the butter and onion and cook over a medium heat for 5–10 minutes until the onion has softened. Add the garlic, ginger, green chillies and curry leaves and simmer for a further few minutes, then add the cumin seeds, cinnamon stick and cardamom. After another 2 minutes, add the tomatoes, salt, turmeric and chilli powder and simmer until you have a rich-looking sauce.

Add the Pakistani carrots and mix well, then cook, covered over a low heat, for a further 20–25 minutes, checking every 5 minutes (you may need a splash of hot water to stop the mixture from sticking to the pan), until the carrots are al dente, and nearly cooked through.

Finally stir in the peas and season by sprinkling the crushed pepper and cloves over. Cover the pan with a lid and simmer over a low heat for 5 minutes.

Serve with the coriander sprinkled over and flatbreads and salad.

GREEN SALAD

2 green peppers
8 leaves of cos lettuce,
  finely shredded
2 celery sticks, finely diced
2 Granny Smith apples,
  sliced into thin
  matchsticks
½ a cucumber, peeled and
  sliced into thin
  matchsticks
25–30 green seedless
  grapes, halved
8 walnuts (optional)

For the dressing
2 tablespoons whipped
  yoghurt
1 tablespoon white wine
  vinegar
1 tablespoon extra virgin
  olive oil
1 teaspoon dried mint
½ teaspoon salt
½ teaspoon cracked black
  pepper

Preheat your oven to 180°C/gas mark 5. Place your green peppers on a baking tray and put in the oven for 20–25 minutes. Once the pepper is cool discard the stem, stalk and seeds, and dice finely.

Put the dressing ingredients into a large bowl and mix together. Add all the salad ingredients, apart from the walnuts, and toss together, making sure everything is coated in the dressing.

Sprinkle the walnuts on top of the salad, and serve.

TURNIPS, POTATOES AND BROCCOLI

Serves 4

1 tablespoon sunflower oil
  or light olive oil
25g butter
1 medium onion, finely
  chopped
2 cloves of garlic, finely
  chopped
20g ginger purée (see page
  273)
2 green chillies, finely
  chopped
½ teaspoon roasted cumin
  seeds (see page 270)
½ x 400g tin of tomatoes
1 teaspoon salt
½ teaspoon ground
  turmeric
¾ teaspoon red chilli
  powder
300g turnips, cut into small
  dice
300g potatoes, cut into
  small dice
10g fresh ginger, julienned
  (cut into matchsticks)
1 teaspoon garam masala
a handful of fresh
  coriander
1 tablespoon vegetable oil
125g purple broccoli
  spears, parboiled for
  1 minute
salt and black pepper

Heat the oil and butter in a pan. Once hot, add the onion and cook for about 5–10 minutes over a low to medium heat stirring every so often. Add the garlic, ginger purée and green chillies and cook for a further 3 minutes. Add the cumin seeds, tinned tomatoes, salt, turmeric and chilli powder, then let everything simmer away for a few minutes.

Add the turnips and lower the heat, then cover the pan with a lid and cook for about 10 minutes. Add some boiling water if your turnips look a bit dry. Add the potatoes and julienned ginger and cook for a further 10 minutes, or until the turnips and potatoes are soft, then add the garam masala and coriander and cook over a very low heat for 1 final minute.

Put a non-stick pan on the heat. Once hot, add the vegetable oil and heat until smoking hot, then carefully add the broccoli spears and sear for 30 seconds on each side. Season with salt and pepper and place on top of the turnips and potatoes. Eat immediately.

Serve with chapatis and salads.

CARROT, POTATO AND PEAS WITH FENUGREEK

Fresh fenugreek is a wonderful herb. You've got to cook it carefully with the onion to get the flavour to develop.

Serves 4

1 tablespoon sunflower oil

25g butter

1 medium onion, finely chopped

4 cloves of garlic, finely chopped

20g fresh ginger, puréed (see page 273)

4 green chillies, finely chopped

½ teaspoon roasted cumin seeds (see page 270)

½ teaspoon roasted fenugreek seeds (see page 270)

45g fresh fenugreek, plus about 15g for garnish

½ x 400g tin of tomatoes

200ml water

1 teaspoon salt

½ teaspoon ground turmeric

400g carrots, cut into 2cm squares

4 medium potatoes, cut into 2cm squares

120g frozen peas

¼ teaspoon garam masala

Oil for deep-frying the fenugreek leaves

Put the oil and butter into a medium pan and place on the heat. Once hot, add the onion and cook gently for 5–10 minutes, then add the garlic, ginger and green chillies. Let everything simmer away for 2 minutes, then add the cumin seeds, fenugreek seeds and fresh fenugreek and cook for 3 minutes, or until the aroma of the fenugreek is quite strong and the tips of the leaves are darker green.

Now add the tinned tomatoes, water, salt and turmeric and cook for a further 3 minutes, then add the carrots. Cover the pan with a lid and reduce the heat to low. After 5 minutes add the potatoes and cook for another 10 minutes, or until the carrots and potatoes are soft. Add the frozen peas and mix well, then add the garam masala. Cover with the lid again and let everything simmer for a few minutes, or until the peas are cooked.

Chop the remaining 15g of fresh fenugreek leaves. Pour enough oil into a small saucepan to come a third of the way up the pan and place over a medium heat. To check it's hot enough for deep-frying, add a pinch of flour to the oil and it should sizzle madly. Deep fry the fenugreek leaves then sprinkle them over the dish.

CARDAMOM RICE PUDDING WITH GINGER CHERRIES

Serves 4–6
180g basmati rice soaked
    for 1 hour
300 ml water
800 ml milk
160g caster sugar
1 tablespoon granulated
    sugar
3 green cardamom pods

For the cherries
250 g cherries, stoned
1 tablespoon water
2 tablespoons caster sugar
1 star anise
2 1-inch pieces of fresh
    ginger finely diced

Put the rice in a very heavy based ovenproof pan (I normally put my pan on top of a griddle to give it more thickness) and add 300ml water. Bring to a simmer, then leave on a very low heat until the rice has absorbed the water. Add the milk, sugar and the cardamom pods. Let everything slowly simmer away for about an hour or until the rice has fully absorbed the milk.

Pre heat your oven to 190C/gas mark 5. Sprinkle about 1 tablespoon of sugar on top of the rice and place into the oven for about 15 minutes or until the sugar becomes caramelised and forms a golden crust.

To marinate the cherries:

Put the water, sugar and star anise into a pan over a moderate heat. Once the sugar starts to caramelise add the ginger, then let it cool it down before adding the cherries. Leave the cherries in the caramel for 3-4 minutes, before carefully fishing out and laying on a sheet of baking parchment to cool.

Once the sugar has caramelised on top of the rice pudding, serve warm sprinkled with a few of your caramelised ginger cherries.

Previously: Two of Monir's great nieces,
up from Birmingham to visit the Scottish
side of the family.

BAKED APPLES WITH CARDAMOM

Serves 4

4 Granny Smith apples
100g brown sugar
½ teaspoon slightly
  cracked black
  peppercorns
seeds from 2 green
  cardamom pods
100g butter, softened
250ml apple juice

Preheat the oven to 200°C/gas mark 7.

Peel and core the apples, then pat them dry with kitchen paper. In a bowl, mix together the sugar, peppercorns and cardamom seeds. Brush the soft butter on to the apples, using a pastry brush, then roll them in the spiced sugar until fully coated.

Place the apples in an ovenproof dish and bake in the oven for 10 minutes, then take them out and add the apple juice. Turn down the oven to 180°C/gas mark 6. Return the apples to the oven for a further 20 minutes, basting them every 5 minutes with the apple juice.

Serve with vanilla ice cream or double cream.

SAFFRON BREAD AND BUTTER PUDDING

Serves 4–6

8 slices of white bread,
  crusts included
50g butter
100g sultanas
200ml full-fat milk
6 strands of saffron
300ml double cream
3 egg yolks
50g sugar
a pinch of grated nutmeg

Preheat the oven to 180°C/gas mark 6 and butter a medium-sized rectangular baking dish.

Butter the bread and cut each slice into 4 small squares. Layer half the bread evenly across the base of the prepared dish, then sprinkle over the sultanas and cover with the remaining bread.

Heat 50ml of the milk in a small saucepan. Once lukewarm, take off the heat and add the saffron and leave to infuse for 10 minutes, giving it a swirl now and then. Mix together the cream, egg yolks, remainder of the milk and sugar and pass through a sieve into a clean bowl. Make sure the saffron-infused milk isn't piping hot, allow it to cool slightly if need be, then add it to the egg mixture. Pour over the buttered bread and grate the nutmeg over the top.

Stand the pudding dish in a larger ovenproof dish or baking tray. Now pour enough hot water into the outside dish to come halfway up the sides of the pudding dish. Bake in the oven for about 35–40 minutes, or until the top is golden and the custard is set.

MINI PARIS BUNS

Paris buns bring back many memories for me. When my dad bought fish for the family on Saturday, he always got some buns from the baker's across from the fishmonger's on the Saltmarket. It was a nice treat washed down with a cup of tea. Paris buns have traditionally been popular in poorer areas of Scotland and Ireland, as they are cheap and filling. I was lucky enough to come across a recipe a few years ago from master baker James Burgess (*The Baker's Tale*).

Makes 25–30

sunflower oil, for greasing
225g self-raising flour
75g butter, cubed
75g caster sugar
2 eggs (1 for glazing)
50g sultanas
100ml milk
50g sugar nibs

Preheat the oven to 200°C/gas mark 7 and lightly grease a non-stick oven tray or baking sheet with sunflower oil.

Sift the flour into a mixing bowl. Rub in the butter until the mixture resembles breadcrumbs, then add the sugar, 1 egg, sultanas and milk and mix well. Form into small round balls roughly the size of a chestnut and place on the greased tray, leaving a 4cm gap between the buns.

Whisk the remaining egg and glaze the buns with it, sprinkle the sugar nibs on top, and bake in the oven for about 15 minutes, or until the buns have risen and are golden brown in colour.

MINT ICE CREAM WITH CHOCOLATE-DIPPED CHERRIES

Serves 4
For the cherries
100g dark chocolate
20 glace cherries

For the ice cream
200ml full-fat milk
300ml double cream
6 sprigs of fresh mint
50g caster sugar
4 large egg yolks,
 preferably free-range

Start with the cherries. Bring a small pan of water to a gentle simmer and carefully place a heatproof bowl on top making sure the bowl doesn't touch the water. Add the chocolate to the bowl and let it slowly melt. Dip the cherries in the melted chocolate and leave to cool down on a tray lined with baking parchment.

Put the milk and cream into a heavy-based pan and bring to boiling point over a high heat. Take off the heat, add the mint sprigs, then set aside to infuse for 30 minutes.

Strain the milk and cream mixture through a sieve into a bowl, pressing the mint leaves with a spoon to get the maximum flavour from them. Discard the mint, then pour the infused milk back into the pan and bring to boiling point.

Whisk together the sugar and egg yolks in a bowl until pale, then pour over half the milk and cream, whisking all the time. Slowly add the remaining milk and cream, then pour the mixture back into the pan and cook over a low heat, stirring all the time, until it thickens like custard. This will take about 3–4 minutes – but be careful not to overheat the mixture as it may curdle. Strain through a sieve into a bowl and leave to cool (stirring occasionally to stop a skin forming), then cover and chill completely in the fridge.

Churn the mixture in an ice cream machine, if you have one, until it's frozen and smooth. If you don't have an ice cream machine, place the mixture in a plastic container and put into the freezer for about 2 hours, whisking it every so often in order to prevent crystals forming.

Serve the mint ice cream in a glass or bowl and top with the cherries. You may like to flake off some of the chocolate from the cherries.

COCONUT BALLS

250g desiccated coconut
1 x 397g tin of condensed
   milk
2 x 200g bars of milk or
   dark chocolate

Put the coconut and condensed milk into a bowl and mix well. Leave to set for an hour, then shape into balls roughly the size of chestnuts.

Put the chocolate into a heatproof bowl over a pan of simmering hot water making sure the base of the bowl doesn't touch the water. Allow to melt.

Coat the coconut balls in the melted chocolate and put on a plate or a wire rack to dry.

Basic Techniques

This is quite an important section to get your head around, especially if you're new to Indian cooking. It'll make life a lot easier if you gather together some basic supplies and get comfortable with a few techniques ahead of attempting the recipes. These will stand you in good stead, whatever you decide to make. This is both a starting point and also something to refer to when you are trying out any of the recipes in the book.

Your larder and spices

These pretty much cover your basic needs for most of the recipes. Don't panic if it seems like a big list. The dried stuff will last for ages, and most of the fresh stuff is readily available.

LONG-LASTING THINGS

Good-quality tinned tomatoes, tomato purée

Curry leaves, cloves, nutmeg, black peppercorns, cinnamon sticks, black cardamoms, green cardamoms

Fennel seeds, cumin seeds, coriander seeds, fenugreek seeds, mustard seeds

Chilli powder, chilli flakes, ground cumin, ground turmeric

Chickpeas, red lentils, chana daal, basmati rice, chapati flour, wholemeal fine gram flour

Tikka and tandoori pastes, honey

FRESH THINGS

Coriander, flat-leaf parsley, mint, fenugreek

Ginger, green chillies, garlic

Onions (the better the quality, the better the result – small organic ones are great)

Useful equipment

Spice box (two if you're feeling flush) – keeps your spices neat and tidy and in one place.

'You must, must, must have a mortar and pestle' (one of our favourite lines from the film *Julie & Julia*)

Mini food processor

Tava or flat griddle

Non-stick pans

Ovenproof pans

Heavy-based pans

Useful techniques

CARAMELISING

Caramelising or browning before you cook gives your ingredients a really deep colour on the outside and adds richness to the flavour.

Heat 1 large tablespoon of vegetable oil in a large pan. Add the ingredients to the pan and ensure that all sides are caramelised. This will take 3–4 minutes. Make sure you don't overcrowd your pan. When cooking, your ingredients will release moisture, and if your pan is too crowded then you will steam rather than brown what you are cooking.

PAN-FRYING AND SEARING

This makes the dish more appealing and also seals in the juices.

Heat up a non-stick pan and add 1 tablespoon olive oil. Once very hot, add the chicken. Sear on one side for 3 minutes, then flip over and sear the other side for 2 minutes.

BASIC BRAISING TECHNIQUES

Braising meat is a useful way of making a less expensive piece of meat softer and more delicious.

Season your meat with a little salt and pepper and other spices if using.

Heat a tablespoon of oil in a large pan and add the meat. Turn regularly to make sure that the meat is brown on all sides.

Once your meat has taken on colour, transfer it to an ovenproof dish. Add your chosen sauce and cook slowly in the oven on a low heat (about 150°C/gas mark 2) for 1½–2 hours.

ROASTING SPICES

It's usually best to keep the spices in your spice tin whole, as once they are crushed they quickly lose their aroma.

Place your chosen spices in a small pan and put them over a gentle heat for about 1–1½ minutes. They will take on a slightly darker colour. You've got to be very careful here, as if they're roasted too long they will burn, and this will produce a bitter taste. Only the mustard seeds should begin to pop in the pan. If anything else pops this means it's burnt. Don't forget to use your sense of smell. Your sensory abilities are very important in cooking. As you practise you will start to make a connection between the smell of perfectly roasted spices and the resulting taste. Take the pan off the heat and allow the spices to cool.

BASIC PESTLE AND MORTAR

There's no simpler job in the kitchen than using your pestle and mortar. It's also a good way to work out some of the day's stresses!

Put the required amount of whole roasted spices into the mortar and bash with the pestle. Make sure you don't grind your spices too finely.

THE RIGHT TIME TO ADD SPICES

Of course every curry is different, but on the whole I tend to add my spices to the pan once the onions are soft.

EXCESS OIL

If you find that the finished dish has excess oil, all you have to do is tilt the dish – this will bring the oil to the bottom of the pot and you can remove it with a large spoon or ladle.

Try out these techniques until you understand the principles and get used to them. With a bit of practice you will develop a more instinctive sense of how to do things, which is really important. It's vital to try to use your sense of smell in order to learn how the right aroma corresponds to the best taste, and getting the order and temperature of things right can help you to build that proper base which is fundamental to achieving the best result.

This can be done beforehand
or when finishing the dish,
depending on your preference.

You will need:
a small steel bowl about 8cm long
    and 2.5cm deep, or a tin foil
    container
a small lump of charcoal,
    about 5cm
4 cloves
1 tablespoon oil (any kind will do)

SMOKING

First you will have to light the small piece of charcoal. There are a couple of ways to do this. If you have a barbecue, put the charcoal in and light it using your preferred method. You can also use a blowtorch, or simply place the charcoal above the flame on a gas hob in an old metal sieve, or on a piece of mesh (be careful of sparks).

When the charcoal is turning white, put it into a small metal dish. If you don't have a suitable dish to hand, you can improvise one using an aluminium takeaway container.

Make a small trough inside the pan of ingredients you want to smoke so that your smoking device can sit in the middle of the mixture, without falling over.

Carefully place the cloves on top of the charcoal and pour on the oil. You will immediately see smoke belting out from your metal smoking dish.

Quickly put the lid back on the pan and leave for 5 minutes. This is a surprisingly effective method for infusing the dish with a delicious aromatic smokiness. After 5 minutes, carefully remove the smoking dish from the pan and discard once cool.

Useful recipes

Garlic Purée

2 bulbs of garlic
2 tablespoons light olive oil

Peel the garlic, then place it in a mini food processor and give it a few whisks until it is finely crushed. Put into a small glass jar or other container and cover with the oil, then put on a lid or cover with clingfilm and place in the fridge until ready to use (it should keep for up to 5 days).

Ginger Purée

150g ginger
2 tablespoons light olive oil

Peel and chop the ginger, then place it in a mini food processor and whisk until it is crushed. Put into a small glass jar or other container and cover with the oil, then put on a lid or cover with clingfilm and place in the fridge until ready to use (it should keep for up to 4 days).

Green Chillies

10 green chillies
2 tablespoons light olive oil

Wash the green chillies, then take off the stalks and pat the chillies dry. Place in a mini food processor and whisk until they are crushed, then put into a small glass jar or other container. Cover with the oil, then put on the lid or cover with clingfilm and place in the fridge until ready to use (it should keep for up to 4 days).

Slow-cooked Onions

5 small to medium onions, finely
   chopped
4 ripe plum tomatoes, chopped
3 green chillies, sliced
120ml water
3 tablespoons light olive oil

Put the onions, tomatoes and chillies into a medium pan and cover with the water. Bring to the boil, then turn down the heat and leave to simmer. Put a lid on the pan, but not fully, leaving a gap for the steam to get out, and let everything simmer away for 90 minutes. (You may need to add a little more water.) Once the water has evaporated, lightly mash the mixture with a potato masher. Let it cool down, then transfer to a container. Pour the olive oil on top and place in the fridge (use within 5 days).

Crispy Onions

350ml vegetable oil for
   deep-frying
4 small white onions, very thinly
   sliced

Crispy onions have a great flavour and can transform a dish. They are particularly good with rice dishes.

Heat the oil in a heavy-based pan and deep-fry the onions until golden in colour. Remove from the pan with a slotted spoon, then drain and spread them out on kitchen paper so that any excess oil can be absorbed.

Oven-cooked Tomatoes

8 ripe plum tomatoes
3 tablespoons olive oil
¼ teaspoon sea salt
¼ teaspoon cracked black pepper
4 cloves of garlic, unpeeled

Preheat the oven to 100°C/gas mark ¼. Cut the tomatoes in half. Take out the stalk, then cut each tomato into 3 equal wedges. Pour the oil into an oven tray, adding the salt and black pepper, then add the tomatoes and garlic. Lightly and carefully massage the oil over the tomatoes. Place in the oven for 6 hours.

Skinning Tomatoes

6 ripe but firm plum tomatoes

Bring a medium pan of water to the boil, making sure it has enough water in it to cover the tomatoes. Score the base of each tomato crossways, as this will make it easier to peel them. Once the water has come to the boil, turn the heat down, then carefully add the tomatoes. After 1 minute turn the heat off. You should see the skin separating from the flesh. With a slotted spoon, take out the tomatoes and leave to cool.

Once cooled, skin the tomatoes, cut out the core, and discard the core and seeds. Chop the flesh, place in the fridge and use within 5 days.

Ghee

250g butter, cut into cubes
1 teaspoon wholemeal flour

Heat the butter in a small pan over a low heat until it comes to a simmer. Let it simmer away for 2 minutes (it will become quite foamy), then add the flour and continue to simmer for about 8 minutes, or until you see the solids becoming golden brown. Take off the heat (don't let the butter become dark brown) and let it stand for 2 minutes, by which time all the solids should have sunk to the bottom. Once it has cooled down, put it through a sieve lined with muslin – the result should be a light golden butter.

Garlic Pickle

¼ teaspoon fennel seeds
¼ teaspoon fenugreek seeds
1 star anise
2 tablespoons olive oil
2 tablespoons brown sugar
½ tablespoon salt
175ml white malt vinegar
3 bulbs of garlic, peeled and finely
    chopped

In a small pan, dry roast the fennel seeds, fenugreek seeds and star anise for about 30 seconds, then add the olive oil. After another 30 seconds add the sugar, salt and vinegar and let everything simmer for about 5 minutes. Take off the heat and let it cool down, then add the garlic and mix well. Transfer into glass jars and leave for a week for all the flavours to combine before using. Half a teaspoon of this will add a kick to any dish.

Raita

Serves 4

300g natural yoghurt

2 baby cucumbers or ½ a regular
cucumber, finely sliced

½ teaspoon salt

½ teaspoon minced green chilli

1 teaspoon dried mint

¼ teaspoon black peppercorns,
crushed

Put the yoghurt into a bowl and give it a good whisk, making sure it is nice and smooth. Add the sliced cucumbers, salt, green chilli and dried mint and mix together, then sprinkle the crushed black peppercorns on top.

Potatoes

Not all dishes have to be served with rice or breads – sometimes it is nice to have an alternative. For example, you can use any kind of potatoes – baby potatoes, mashed potatoes, boiled potatoes, a comforting roast potato or delicious chips.

Roast Potatoes

1kg Cyprus potatoes

salt, to taste

100ml sunflower oil

4 cloves of garlic, unpeeled

2 sprigs of fresh rosemary

Peel the potatoes and cut each one into quarters. Parboil them in a pan with enough salted water to barely cover them.

Preheat the oven to 200°C/gas mark 6. Pour the oil into a large roasting tin and put it into the oven to heat up. Once the potatoes are boiled, drain them in a colander, then carefully place them in the hot oil. They will sizzle as they go in. Turn them and roll them around so they are covered with the oil. Add the garlic cloves and the rosemary.

Roast the potatoes for 15 minutes, then take them out of the oven and turn them over. Put them back into the oven and roast for a further 10–20 minutes, or until they are golden and crispy.

Garam Masala

1 tablespoon cumin seeds

12 cloves

20 black peppercorns

2 black cardamoms

1 large cinnamon stick

Heat a pan over a low to medium heat. Add all the ingredients and dry roast for about 1 minute, or until the cumin seeds darken slightly. Once cool, either transfer to a mortar and bash with the pestle into a rough powder, or use a small spice grinder. Store in a small container with a lid.

Green Chilli Pickle

50ml mustard oil

20 green poblano chillies (available in Asian food stores), washed, dried and stalks removed

1 tablespoon salt

Heat the mustard oil in a small pan. Once slightly warm, add the chillies and simmer on a low heat for about 8 minutes, stirring all the time, until the chillies soften and the colour turns a lighter green. Turn the heat off and leave to cool. Stir in the salt, then transfer to a glass jar. Turn the jar upside down every few days, making sure the salt dissolves. The pickle will be ready to use in 4 days.

Smoked Aubergines

about 12 baby aubergines, halved
4 cloves
2 tablespoons oil

Put the aubergines into a pan with a tight-fitting lid, leaving a bit of space for the steel container (don't use your best pan, as sometimes the smoke lingers). Put your steel container into the pot with the aubergines. Light the charcoal and wait until it is pretty hot (about 10 minutes), then put the hot charcoal into the steel container. Carefully place the cloves on top and pour over the oil (at this point smoke will start to come out). Quickly put the lid on the pan and leave it for about 15 minutes, to let the aubergines smoke.

Sometimes we smoke the finished dish once cooked and off the heat (e.g. Smoked Lamb Chops and Broccoli, page 118), making a small space in the pot and using the same procedure above.

The authors would like to thank their families for all their help, love and support over the years.

Thank yous also go to the following people, listed alphabetically:

John Adam and Susie, Dave Addison, Allan and Joe, Dr Ashfaq and Rashida, Ryan B, Iain Banks, Gill Barker, Lyndsay Bell, Biff and the band, Jered Bolton, Loretta Boyd, Ian Burnett, David Campbell, Iain Carson, Jim Connelly, Myles Cooney, Dan Docherty, Teresa Docherty, Trevor Dolby, David Eldridge, Alex Findlay, Imogen Fortes, Valerie Fry, Alasdair Gray, Colin Gray, Tim Horrox, Signe Johanssen, Oliver Johnson, Ketan, Niall Lockman, Niki Longmuir, Liana Marletta, Amar Kumar Maurya, The Glasgow Film Theatre, Alan Mawn, Eileen McGhee, Katherine Murphy, Andy Neil, Scott Nicol and family, the Randev family, Margaret Ritchie, Tom Shields, Richard Thornburn, Jerry Whyte, all Amaan's carers, Raquib, Diane, Lucy, Angie, and Isabell, Audrey, Colin and Carol, Diane and Bell, Fiona and Brian, Gary and Helen, Gus and Lynn, Helen and Mal, Nicki, Pete and Dolly, Rose and Ruthie, Ros and Claire, Sid and the Berrys, Tam and the boys, Dai and Jenny Vaughan.

Some of the photographs in this book are also part of Martin Gray's personal project, 'A Sideways Glance' having been used in publications and exhibited in urban public art initiatives as well as interior spaces around the British Isles.

INDEX

Published by Preface 2014

10 9 8

First published in Great Britain in 2014 by
Preface Publishing
20 Vauxhall Bridge Road
London, SW1V 2SA

An imprint of The Random House Group Limited
www.penguin.co.uk

Addresses for companies within The Random House Group Limited
can be found at www.global.penguinrandomhouse.com

The Random House Group Limited Reg. No. 954009

A CIP catalogue record for this book is available from the British Library

ISBN 978 1 848 09442 0

www.greenpenguin.co.uk

Penguin Random House is committed to a sustainable future for our business, our readers and our planet. This book is made from Forest Stewardship Council® certified paper.

Typeset and designed by Two Associates

Photographs © Martin Gray

Colour reproduction by Altaimage London

Printed in China